Understanding People

Ministry To All Stages Of Life

by
Cheryl Fawcett, Ph.D.

Associate Professor of Christian Education
Christian Heritage College, El Cajon, California

Evangelical Training Association

110 Bridge Street • Box 327

Wheaton, IL 60189-0327

Cover Design: Kurtz Design Studio, Tulsa, OK

2001 Edition, Fifth Printing

ISBN: 978-0-910566-99-5

Contents

Preface

A summer vacation sometimes takes a family to an unknown destination. Before the journey has begun maps are consulted, AAA is queried, and friends or coworkers who have been there before are interviewed. One reason for all the preparations is to be as knowledgeable as possible for the coming adventure. Talking with those that have forged on before us to find out the many points of interest, the problem areas to avoid and how to best enjoy the journey as well as the destination is key to the journey. With every precaution taken to know the path ahead, there are still dynamic changes which cannot be predetermined and can either add to the mystery of the hunt or be the disappointment of the journey. Nothing ever goes exactly as planned. So why bother planning the journey just to watch plans change? As with any endeavor, the changes will be less troublesome if one knows what to expect.

For the believer, life is a journey from the mind of God to eternity with God. Life is a fascinating journey that begins with a vision in the mind and heart of God, followed by the miracle of conception, continuing through childhood and adolescence and concluding with the long passage called adulthood. Many are the similarities along the way and so it is wise to learn from others who have not only traveled the road before, but have given special attention to the process of growth and development. Developmental psychologists devote their lives to the study and understanding of (in Kathleen Berger's words) the "usual patterns of growth and change that everyone follows to some degree and that no one follows exactly."

As Christians, we study the intricacies of growth and development in order to positively influence every individual we come in contact with, believer and unbeliever, to become as wholly complete as possible. Jesus said it this way, " I am come that they might have life and that they might have it more abundantly (John 10:10)."

To truly understand people we must blend reading what other specialists have written with our continual observance of people of all ages, and a study of Scripture for the Creator's perspective. This book endeavors to guide you on your journey. It is our desire that you understand people more fully so that you can minister more powerfully in their lives. The insights gained from this pursuit will enhance your ministry skills and should never be used to merely label people or age groups. Each part of life's journey should be enjoyed for what it is, a part of the journey toward maturity and Christ–likeness.

C. L. F.

Understanding Human Development

1

Welcome to the journey! Prepare yourself for exciting insights and challenging thoughts. While each remaining chapter in this volume will address a specific age level, this chapter will discuss the process of development, the periods of development and conclude with an overview of three problems or dilemmas regarding human development. Grab your Bible and let's begin.

Process of Development

Every adult was once an adolescent. Every adolescent was once a child. Every child was once an infant and toddler. Every infant was once a single male sperm that joined with a female ovum or egg. Young adults have children to rear. Senior adults have children and grandchildren to enjoy. Adults can leave a legacy of secrets and truths about life's journey. They can also share the treasures they have discovered in their own personal life journey and from the great guidebook for all humans, the Bible.

While there are many variations in the smaller steps of individual development, the ultimate journey is predictable for all human beings. Our Creator, God, designed the pattern from the very beginning of time (Genesis 1:26). In His creation, the Creator reflects His intentions and purpose. God said that mankind was to be made in His image and likeness (Genesis 1:26). The universe is the result of God's creative design and handiwork; however, the crowning act of His work was the creation of male and female. He declared them "very good" (Genesis 1:31): to Adam and Eve, the first parents, God gave the purpose of being fruitful, increasing in number, filling and sub-duing the earth (Genesis 1: 26–28).

Humans alone were the recipients of the breath of God. All cre-ated beings were made from the dust of the ground (Genesis 2:7), but mankind alone is a living being with an immaterial part that responds to and finds its completion in God. God's mandate of care and supervision was not given to the trees or the animals, but to the man and his "completer." Humans are valuable because God created them with the highest degree of correlation to Himself. Further, to mankind alone came the instructions to manage and care for the earth. Finally, God pursued an intimate relationship, with mankind alone, of walking and talking daily.

Development meant growth in God's original design. Adam and Eve were to work and keep the garden. When Eve and then Adam vio-lated the instructions of God by eating the one fruit that was forbid-den, they caused the curse of God on Satan, themselves and ulti-mately all the earth. Death and decay are the result of the sin of mankind (Genesis 3:14–19). These effects will be reversed one day in the future through God's redemption of not only mankind, but the heavens and the earth as well, and He will then create a new heaven and new earth (Revelation 21:1). Until then we live in a world that progresses in development but is ultimately heading to-ward physical death.

From the world of developmental psychology, we learn that the growth process is a complex intertwining of three identifiable pro-cesses: the biological, the cognitive and the socioemotional compo-nents.[1] The biological processes involve physical changes in individuals including inherited genetic codes from parents, brain development, height and weight changes, motor skills, and hormonal changes throughout the life span. Cognitive processes involve changes in the way an individual thinks, gains knowledge and expresses that knowl-edge through language. Socioemotional processes include those changes that describe the varied ways individuals build relationships with each other, develop and express emotions and develop their unique personality. A good way to visualize the interaction of these processes is to picture them as intersecting and overlapping circles.

For the Christian trying to understand the complete process of development, the spiritual domain must be added. No discussion of development is complete without the spiritual dimension of one's life. This domain interacts with and influences the other three de-scribed above. An individual cannot fully develop until he is devel-oping in his spiritual relationship with God. For the Christian, the spirit comes alive in the process of redemption; for the unbeliever, the spirit lies dead but is in need of rebirth. Luke 2:52 reinforces this idea with its terse summary of the development of Jesus as a human stating that, "Jesus grew in wisdom [cognitive] and stature [biological] and in favor with God [spiritual] and men [socioemotional]."

Each of the four domains has a primary corresponding theorist from whom much can be learned. As Psalm 19:1–6 indicates, much can be learned about God by studying His creatures and His creation. While Scripture always stands as the final word on any theory, much can be known of God's most complex creation, man, from a careful and scientific study of human behavior. From Jean Piaget we learn much regarding the patterns of development in the cognitive domain. From Erik Erickson's eight stages of developmental growth we gain helpful insights regarding the socioemotional development that all individuals pass through over a lifetime. Lawrence Kohlberg opens windows of insight into the ways that humans develop in their moral decision making skills. Kohlberg's three levels and six stages of moral development strongly parallel Piaget's cognitive developmental stages. Finally, from James Fowler comes a description of the stages of faith development. Fowler proposes that at each age level the nature and description of how one believes changes and matures.

In subsequent chapters, each theory will be brought to bear on the particular stage of development being discussed. Building a Christian perspective of development involves always choosing to use the principles of Scripture as final judge and jury when considering theorists' claims. When man's theories move outside the boundaries of God's revealed truth in the Bible they will be amended accordingly.

Periods of Development

Even though human development is more like a seamless garment than a quilt of many individual pieces, for the purpose of investigation we will be subdividing the life span into smaller descriptive segments. The three larger categories of the human life span under which the many small segments are clustered are childhood, adolescence and adulthood. Popularly used divisions include: prenatal (conception to birth) and infancy (birth to twenty four months), toddlers (two years to three years), preschool (four to five years), early childhood (six to eight years), preteen (nine to eleven years), early adolescence (twelve to thirteen years), middle adolescence (fourteen to seventeen years), later adolescence (eighteen to twenty-one), early adult (twenty–two to forty), middle adult (forty–one to sixty–five), and senior adult (sixty–five plus).

While in current times we have subdivided the life span into the three categories of children, youth and adults, for much of recorded history and even in many cultures today around the world there have been only two. There were only two biblical age distinctions: children and adults. In Judaism, a twelve year old male was given a bar mitzva and became a legal adult. In a similar manner, once girls experienced their first menstrual period they were considered to be a woman and the father began to arrange a marriage. Scripture describes these two age divisions in 1 Corinthians 13:11 when it explains, "when I was a child, I talked like a child, I thought like a child, I reasoned like a child. When I became a man, I put childish ways behind me." One was either a child or an adult. In many ways this approach helped individuals take their place more easily in the adult world. Surely there was some hesitation on the part of the novice adult but the advantage was that they were treated like an adult with the appropriate responsibilities and privileges that accompany such status.

In viewing life this way, childhood becomes a time of preparation for the responsibilities and privileges of adulthood. Adolescence serves as the bridge of transition between the two: childhood and adulthood. Around the world, this simpler two segment orientation still dominates the growth process and cultural perspective. However in the highly industrialized cultures of the world, the bridge of transition between childhood and adulthood becomes elongated into a temporary and sometimes permanent destination. We call this phenomenon adolescence. Stalled on the bridge, many adolescents are lingering between the freedom of childhood and the responsibilities of adulthood. Many of the problems associated with youth are the result of postponing adult status and responsibilities for teens.

Problematic Considerations of Development

While much is fairly straightforward in discerning developmental stages and phases, some issues continue to be troublesome for scientists. We will briefly present the issues with the desire that you engage in classroom discussion regarding your perspectives and observations on these matters.

Nature vs. Nurture

This discussion has been raging for centuries and promises to continue to do so in the future. The discussion centers around two key questions: Which is more influential in the growth and development of persons, their hereditary blueprint (genetic makeup) or their environmental circumstances? Which is primary and which is secondary?

Ultimately the answer is a matter of emphasis. The two are so closely linked that it seems nearly impossible to isolate one from the other. Nature and nurture each contribute significantly in the formation of every individual. Surely the nature of a person's parents influence many things about their physical makeup, their racial features, their ultimate height, their eye color, their intellect, and even some predispositions to certain diseases. Much of our physical appearance can be traced to our lineage. On the other hand, nurturing factors and forces definitely influence development by assisting or hindering individual growth. The nature of one's nutrition, the availability and quality of health care and the exposure to diseases contribute much to the individual's final development. Improper nutrition, inadequate health care, multiple calamities, along with prenatal and childhood diseases, can likewise hinder or stop proper growth. In addition to the physical elements of an individual's growth, nurturing influences of family, peers, school, community, government, media and culture add individual and collective influences to a life's formation.

Development is both an internal and an external process. The internal growth is largely a function of heredity at work. The nurture aspects are often initially felt externally by the individual but eventually bear evidence in both internal and external ways. There are myriads of forces outside a person that impact what and whom one becomes. Urie Bronfenbrenner emphasizes an ecological approach to the study of development.[2] His schematic is similar to the layers of an onion each of which contributes its own influences upon the developing person. Closest to the center and having the most profound influence are the microsystems of the family, the peer group, one's religious setting, classroom or workplace. Brofenbrenner's next layer includes the mesosystems that connect the microsystems. As the family and religious setting interface, the Sunday School teacher and parent interact to work together for the spiritual growth of a child. As the classroom and family interact, the teacher and parent strive together to maximize the child's educational progress. Exosystems come in the next layer and influence the mesosystems. Exosystems include school systems, medical institutions, mass media, and community makeup. Their influence is important but exerts less impact than that of microsystems. The final or outer layer of the schematic includes those macrosystems which impact and formulate the individual indirectly. Cultural values, social conditions, economic patterns, political philosophy, and natural customs comprise the most distant layer and provide the context in which growth and development take place.

An example of Brofenbrenners model can be seen in the following fictional but possible scenario. A child is born into a postmodern relative culture of the new millennium. Amid the multicultural city of Metropolis, he grows up in the inner city projects. Historically, his is a time of political liberalism and dominance of the the country's highest government officials. While it will be years before he understands any of these influencers on his growth, each will nonetheless influence the person he will become. Furthermore, if that child is raised with much access to violent video games, is initiated into a local gang, is educated in an under funded deteroriating public school with poorly trained teachers, his life will reflect those influences. Finally, if that child is born into a single parent family on welfare with an absentee or noninvolved father, his chances of growing up to love and serve God seem all but impossible. However, if into this child's life enters an Inner City Impact parachurch ministry that seeks to service the child, his education, his peers and ultimately his soul with the good news of Jesus, that child has a fighting chance to grow up to be a full individual. He begins the journey as he establishes friendships with caring adults, learns better study habits, and forms healthy friendships outside of gangs. Additionally, if he hears the truth of the gospel, and is challenged toward salvation, he has the opportunity to choose Christ as Savior and Lord of his life. All this begins with his Inner City Impact counselor. Ultimately, he can become involved in the family of God through a local church. Through that church family, this child can build a healthy relationship with a caring godly adult male who models to him what a man of God acts like. Many are the systems that influence this child and his development. Despite all the disadvantages of the surrounding systems of this child's development, he becomes a fully developed and functioning adult because of the influence of Christian education in his life.

This is good news for the Christian educator. While some developmental boundaries are set because of heritage, others can be influenced by godly parenting, interaction with a faith community, and biblical training of God's timeless values and principles. In fact, Christian education can actually reverse some of the negative impact of social environmental formation. Moses rightly reminds parents in Deuteronomy 6 of the key role they play in the spiritual formation of their children. Parents were first to internalize the commandments into their own hearts and then to impress them upon the children everywhere and anywhere they could. Even though sin has deeply scarred and impaired man's perception, God's word can restore right thinking and right living to the one who chooses to learn and live its truths.

Continuity vs. Discontinuity

The second debated issue in developmental circles is whether development is a series of small incremental steps or big jumps of growth.

Is it a set of stairs or a gradual incline? Do you awaken on your second birthday to find you have acquired an entire vocabulary fit for making sentences overnight? Do you walk into preschool to discover you now have new powers of learning that you previously did not possess? When you awaken on your thirteenth birthday, have you miraculously become a teenager? When you turn sixty–five does your body automatically kick into the declining mode readying you for the next life?

Is growth a gradual increase in quantity of intellectual, socioemotional, and biological changes or is it ultimately a qualitative process in which different and distinctive kinds of growing take place? Are there distinct stages or is the process of growth and development so incremental that it happens without one noticing the progression?

Understanding people is ultimately understanding the answers to these questions. Yes, we grow in such small increments that at times we are unaware of the changes taking place. Remember your grandmother's "My how you've grown" greetings? Remember how you resented that greeting? You were not aware of the subtle changes taking place even though you lived inside the body and mind that were changing. But Grandma, having not seen you in a while, could detect the quantitative as well as qualitative growth you were experiencing. Grandma had the big picture while you were lost in the day to day micro changes that were at work in you.

So is development essentially quantitative (more of the same kind), or qualitative (of a different kind)? The answer is that both are true. You are making small changes as you grow and develop, but you are also experiencing some changes that are so profound the essence of your person changes forever. This book endeavors to focus on both kinds of growth.

The implications of quantitative and qualitative growth among learners in church educational settings will be introduced in each domain of development for each age level. In the outset, let us set the stage by saying that we must learn to adjust our teaching so that as students change and develop, our strategies will be the best suited to them at each particular stage of their lives. At the same time, we must also plan for bigger changes in ministry focus as students move from children's ministry to youth or adult ministries.

Descriptive vs. Predictive Formation

A final area of discussion, within the developmentalist perspective, revolves around how predictive the early influences are on the life of a growing individual. Do those influences provide a description of the child or a prescription of what they must become? Can the natural processes be interrupted or refocused?

Will either neglect or over parenting cripple a child for life? Does an alcoholic prenatal environment limit the potential outcome of a child's ability to learn and be fully developed? Do children reared in war zones become emotionally and socially crippled for life? Some developmentalists believe that a child will never attain optimal growth unless he or she has experienced a warm, nurturant care giving in the first year of life. Fortunately for Christian educators in the church and home, another perspective is that children remain malleable throughout development and that sensitive care giving received later in life is just as important as earlier sensitive care giving. So we are not robots whose exitstence is programmed and predetermined by specific events, but we are living human beings whose formation has many influencers. We are not doomed but redeemable!

Conclusion

Development is normal; it is God–given and is similar yet unique in each individual. Life is precious and to be cherished. Much can be learned by keen observational skills, reading appropriate literature, and searching the Bible for insights. Life span is divided into three major sections: childhood, adolescence and adulthood. Each individual experiences growth in biological, cognitive, socioemotional and spiritual ways. The more one knows of the developmental pathway the better equipped one is to accomplish ministry in the life of students.

Notes

1. John W. Santrock, *Psychology*, sixth ed. (Boston: McGraw Hill, 2000), 320-321.
2. See a discussion of Bronfenbrenner's approach in Kathleen Stassen Berger's, *The Developing Person Through the Life Span*, fourth ed. (New York, NY: Worth Publishers, 1998), 1.

Discussion Questions

1. Identify and explain the significant contributions of the follow ing developmental theorists: Piaget, Erickson, Kohlberg, and Fowler.
2. Name the two major divisions of life that scripture outlines and compare with that the three segments that modern culture out lines.

Application Activities

1. Collect recent stories from newspapers or magazines that indicate human life in childhood, adolescence or adulthood.
2. Identify two practical ways the family, school, church, peer group, and society can influence the development of a person.

Prenatal – 24 Months

2

Holly knew that the news of her pregnancy was supposed to be good news. She had desired a baby for three years now. Holly and her husband, Dean, were both young professionals who had earned college degrees as well as having launched their individual careers. Their marriage four years ago had been a storybook event with all their loved ones in attendance sharing the special inauguration of their life together. They had quickly acclimated to living together and sharing their newfound life of oneness.

This baby was a huge step for them both. Holly knew that her life would change with the arrival of this little one in dramatic and significant ways. She welcomed the changes but was still nervous as she contemplated what this might mean to her individually, professionally and in her relationship with Dean. Dean greeted the news with calm reserve. He too wrestled with the implications of being responsible for rearing a child to know and love God in this sin ravaged world. He wondered if he was up to the task of being a dad when he was still finding his bearings as a husband, provider and protector. God's help would surely be necessary if he were to do well as a parent.

Pre-Journey Interventions

Prenatal Development Ministry Implications – Care and Support

New parents find themselves immersed in a world of new terminology. The scientific names of the stages for the beginning of life are conception (one second in time), germinal period (two weeks after fertilization), embryonic period (three to eight weeks), and fetal period (two to seven months). The miracle of birth is overshadowed only by the tremendous growth that occurs to bring a life into the world; from the size of the dot over an "i" to nearly twenty inches long and six pounds! Now that is God's miraculous design at work.

Bible believers value life as a gift from God. David beautifully describes in Psalm 139: 13–16, the process whereby he was formed in the womb. While this beautiful piece of artistic work is literally accomplished in the mother's womb, David acknowledges God's hand in each and every aspect of the production. David's affirmation gives dignity, purpose and direction to life.

In modern times, much has been learned through study of the prenatal stages. The potential dangers for the baby are many as he/she relates to the mother's choices during this critical time of development. The mother's health has direct impact on the life of the unborn child. An HIV–infected mother has a significant chance of passing the deadly disease to her child through the placenta during delivery, and/or after birth through breast–feeding. Fetal alcohol syndrome (FAS) is a cluster of abnormalities that occur in children born to mothers who drink heavily during pregnancy. More recent studies open the possibility that even small amounts of alcohol can harm the forming child. Expectant mothers who smoke similarly heighten the possibility of fetal and neonatal deaths and pre–term delivery for forming children. Mothers should be immunized against German measles, and should avoid X–rays, toxic chemicals, sexually transmitted diseases and other drugs as each can cause serious damage to a pre–born baby. Helping the expectant mother to take responsibility for herself and her unborn child requires loving support, especially for the teenage mother who is barely more than a child herself. Once conception occurs, focus shifts to protecting the unborn life. Abstinence, however, is an important topic to teach teenagers,

Worldwide ministries exist with the purpose to intervene for the life of the unborn. Crisis Pregnancy Centers (CPC), run by volunteers, express love for the unborn child as well as single pregnant women who find themselves in a physical, moral and spiritual crisis. Reports of young expectant women coming to Christ as Savior through the caring intervention of a concerned and involved believer are many. Lives are saved both in the literal and eternal sense.

A Journey Well Begun is Half Done

Biological Ministy Implications

Pre-mature babies experience numerous complications as they enter the world: lungs and other bodily organs may not be completely formed, they are more susceptible to illnesses and they tend to require longer hospital periods than healthy, full–term babies. Parents are thrust into the world of the neonatal intensive care unit. White lab coats, incubators, tubes, and other medical equipment provide emotional challenges for the parents. Ministries of presence are key. Caring for other children already in the home frees the parents to make daily trips to the hospital. Providing meals and completing chores lighten the load of already overwhelmed parents and demonstrate the love of Jesus in tangible, sacrificial ways.

Full-term babies inaugurate the constant flow in physical development. These changes are staggering for newborns; sleeping twenty hours each day changes rapidly into the ability to push themselves up with baby arms, roll over, sit up, stand and walk. These motor skill milestones are landmarks along the pathway of gross motor development. At birth, a child's brain contains approximately 100 billion nerve cells—virtually all the nerve cells he is going to have in his entire life. At birth the neurons are only minimally connected but as the child grows the interconnections increase dramatically. Interaction with the physical and tangible world facilitates the making of these connections. Numerous brightly colored soft plastic toys are essential. Picture books made of fabric are helpful for stimulation. Mobiles and stacking toys allow infants to explore and learn about their world.

Nurseries must provide adequate care for newborns with ample supply of cribs for sleeping. Diaper changing stations, access to water for hand washing, and plenty of room for crawlers and walkers is also key. In fact, as children approach two years they are so adept at walking and running that to meet their need is to provide the most space available to accomodate the progress toward standing and walking.

Growing is the infant's chief task. Endless rounds of eating, sleeping and exercising enhance the infant's growth and development. Large quantities of human touch has also been documented to improve growth, health, and well–being of infants. Plenty of loving hands attached to caring adults make the nursery a place of viable ministry for infants. Snacks and extra diapers are standard equipment for this classroom. The ratio of workers to children should be as close to one adult for every two children as possible to ensure that each child is safely held, fed, changed and loved. Children in their first two years reach half their adult height and one fifth of their adult weight.

Cognitive Ministry Implications

Much of what we know regarding the cognitive development of individuals comes from the careful observations of Swiss psychologist, Jean Piaget. In the 1960s, Piaget's ideas were imported to the United States to assist our understanding of how children actively construct their cognitive world in a series of predictable stages. Most learning is identified as happening through the process of *assimilation*, involving an individual incorporating new information into existing knowledge, especially when the learner is only months old. Not all new information however fits into one's existing knowledge. When information does not fit the existing structure, *accomodation* takes place as the learner finds new ways of understanding.[1]

Infants explore their world unceasingly. From birth to age two their mode of learning is described by Piaget as the *sensorimotor stage*; learning by coordinating sensory experiences (tastes, smell, touch) with motor actions.

At five months, a child literally perceives that an object "out of sight" is literally "out of mind." Three months later, an object hidden from view will be pursued because the child now understands that objects have permanence and continue to exist even though they can not be seen, heard, or touched. Hiding a toy is another way to stimulate the cognitive development of these little ones.

In a ministry setting, this means that a variety of colorful, soft, nontoxic toys and real world items need to be available. Children should hear words like, "Touch this! Try this. Oh what is this? How does that taste?" Gone should be the warnings of do not touch, do not feel, do not explore or do not climb on that. Cleanliness and sanitation are real challenges for the nursery worker who would create a safe place for a child to be exposed to the many things that God has created. Proper sanitation will necessitate washing toys and hands frequently, changing sheets, and possibly having a nurse on duty in the nursery. A room for nursing mothers, with a monitor broadcasting the adult worship services, is another way to say to moms, "We want you here and we want to make your life a little easier."

Socioemotional Ministry Implications

The chief theorist in the socioemotional domain is Erik Erickson. Trained in Europe, Erickson came to the United States to teach at Harvard University. He believed and taught that personality, while greatly formed and shaped in the first five years of life, actually requires a lifetime to attain its full process of development.[2] Each stage or phase in Erickson's model represents a crisis of sorts that results in either increased vulnerability and stunted growth on the part of the individual or enhanced potential for successful accomplishment of the task. There are eight stages all together, four that should be crossed in childhood, one in adolescence and three in adulthood. Each will be discussed in the following appropriate chapters.

Stage one, according to Erickson, occurs during the first year of life and is titled, *trust versus mistrust*. As a child's most basic need of comfort, food and care are met, the child develops a belief that the world is a good place and can be trusted. Conversely, when a child's most basic needs are not met the child learns distrust and thus concludes that the world is a bad place and people are not worthy of trust. The story is told of a child that came to a foster family who did not cry. The child stared aimlessly into space and did not respond to any motion, sound or attention that the caring family tried to provide. When they checked with the social worker who placed the child in their home, they were informed that the child's first residence had been with a working single mother who would leave the child home alone for eight hours a day with only a bottle nearby. The child's cries for help, comfort and love were not met, thus the child had ceased even crying. That child had learned a deep and penetrating lesson of mistrust. As devastating as that true account is, the more exciting news is that with consistent and persistent care of the infant's needs, the baby recovered within a year and continued to develop normally. Praise God for a family that was willing to share the love of God with a socially and emotionally wounded newborn!

A nursery ministry that will assist in the socioemotional development of newborns will adequately staff its nursery with loving adults, both male and female, who are trained to carefully and lovingly respond to the child's cries for help. The nursery is no place for extended conversations between adult workers but rather it is a place that is intently focused on meeting the physical, emotional and spiritual needs of its young ones. Yes, infants demand a lot of time and attention, but they are at a vital stage, learning whether or not people and the world can be trusted. At this time in their young lives, they are learning to trust the adults in their lives to meet their needs. It is not just about rocking babies and changing diapers: nursery ministry is about building trust so the message of Christ will be heard!

From ages one to three, if the *trust versus mistrust stage* has been resolved, the socioemotional developmental focus shifts to *autonomy versus shame and doubt stage*. A healthy child develops a sense of independence and autonomy. Thus, the toddler's cry of 'I do it myself' is actually a reassuring sign that emotional growth is underway. In the process of seeking autonomy, the child has a necessity to assert his/her own will. The careful parent shapes the will without crushing it, as Dr. James Dobson has asserted in his book, *The Strong Willed Child*. Parents must restrain the child without punishing too harshly. Children must learn the boundaries of what is acceptable and what is not, but if they are continuously disciplined and told not to do/say something, they will not develop properly in this area.

Titus 2 instructs the older women to teach the younger women how to love their children and how to be keepers at home. Surely this admonition has implications for the women of our churches as they lovingly impart lessons learned to young mothers. In so doing, much grief can be spared by both the new parent and the developing child. Classes on parenting skills and young mother's clubs, such as Mothers of Preschoolers (MOPS), are all ways to facilitate the flow of information between generations. A church must be intent on connecting the generations and not assuming that this interconnectedness will happen automatically.

Young children are very sensitive to the sounds and atmosphere around them. Even before they are born, unborn children respond to music, calmness, or agitated and argumentative environments. Fear of strangers is common, as is fear of unfamiliar situations, loud noises, and confusion. Stranger anxiety is common in seven to nine month olds. Adjusting to new environments and new people may take several days or weeks. A sensitive Christian education staff would do its best to provide continuity of nursery workers especially for the children of this age. Parents need to be assured that temporary crying may be necessary as the child becomes accustomed to the nursery and the activities there. A well organized nursery will create a welcoming place for the toddler to enter so as to lessen fearfulness on the part of the toddler. Rocking chairs, carpeted areas, warm lighting and pleasant music all help imitate a home environment and will assist in making a child's transition to the church nursery a less troublesome one. Because the world of the infant or toddler is so limited, it is incumbent on the Christian education staff to provide familiar faces. Since children of this age characteristically play alone or enjoy interaction with caring adults, the staff should proactively interact and initiate playtime. Familiar rituals of snacks, rest time, play time and story time are all useful in conducting a nursery ministry that is positive in its impact on the young ones.

Spiritual Ministry Implications

Infants and toddlers sense and imitate their parents' and teachers' attitudes long before they can learn from any information they may teach. So more than anything this phase of spiritual development is "caught" rather than taught. That fact makes ministry to this age level crucial, for attitudes once learned are hard to change.

Because of their developing cognitive powers, moral judgments are not possible; however, the precursor attitudes that underlay them are being formulated. Parents will foremost mold the attitudes of these little ones towards God, church, the Bible and others around them. Caring adults in the family of God should be allowed to come alongside to influence and reinforce the parent's perspectives. While it is the parents' responsibility to see that the spiritual instruction of their children is accomplished, they are not required to do this task alone. Wise is the parent that enlists the help of others in the faith community. In biblical times, families were nearly always extended families of up to one hundred and fifty people. The nuclear family is an invention of the twentieth century and an unhealthy one for spiritual, social and emotional growth. Yes, parents are responsible but they are not to do it alone. God designed that we support one another as a community of faith.

James Fowler describes the first stage of faith development as that of undifferentiated faith. He says, ". . . at birth we are thrust into a new environment for which we have potential but not yet fully viable abilities. For another nine months after birth we are more dependent on the care of those who nurture us than are all but a few of our mammalian companions . . . The activation and elaboration of our adaptive capacities depends both on the progress of our overall maturation and on the way the persons and conditions of our environment greet us and beckon us into interaction. If there is not enough holding, rocking or stimulating communication, our adaptive capacities for relationship and loving attachments can be severely retarded or non activated."[3] As Fowler continues describing this pre–stage of faith development, he contends that the seeds of trust, courage, hope and love are fused in this stage of an individual's life. If the infant's world consists of abandonment, inconsistency, and deprivation then all that comes later will be threatened. These positive qualities are learned in relationship with the primary care givers in a child's life. Fowler offers the visual for this stage as a mother providing love and care to the newborn cradled in her arms. However, it takes both a mother and a father to thoroughly rear a child. Fathers should love their babies knowing that how babies learn to trust their fathers now, will determine the ease in which they learn to trust their heavenly Father later on.

Parents and local church nursery workers have a significant task, more than changing diapers and the giving of bottles to quiet the crying infant. Their task is to provide an environment in which the babies can learn to trust, to be a source of courage for the little ones, and to be a giver and example of unconditional love.

Notes

1. See explanation of Piaget's ideas in John Santrock, *Psychology*, sixth ed. (Boston, MA: McGraw Hill, 2000), 331-332.
2. See full discussion of Erickson's stages in Santrock, 336-337.
3. James Fowler, *Stages of Faith: the Psychology of Human Development and the Quest for Meaning* (San Francisco, CA: Harper and Row, 1981), 120.

Discussion Questions

1. Describe the development of infants in four or five words: physically, intellectually, emotionally, socially, and spiritually.
2. Why is activity so important in the growth and development of infants?
3. Why is nurture and meeting basic needs such an important parental function?
4. What are some of the values of church ministry to this group?
5. What are the main purposes of the church's ministry for the parents?
6. Name three elements that you believe are vital to ministry to these little ones.
7. How would you describe the ideal worker to infants? Name three men and three women from your congregation that possess those traits.

Application Activities

1. Interview the director of the infant and toddler ministry in your church to discover how the needs of the young child are met through this ministry.
2. Make a list of topics which could be developed into training classes for parents of infants and toddlers.
3. Role play a visit of a staff member, or visitation team, to the home of a prospective couple in your community welcoming them and their infant into the ministry.

Toddlers: Two & Three Years

3

Never underestimate the capacity of a toddler! Producers of Sesame Street, Barney, and Mr. Rogers know they have ability to teach and influence. Just try walking down the toy isle with items targeted toward twos and threes and your toddler will do the rest. "Mommy, me want Mickey!" "My Bert, My Ernie!" The most exciting new development for this age level is the growing ability to communicate. A virtual vocabulary explosion happens to these young ones.

Far from being occupied and out of sight, these little ones are like sponges soaking up songs, words, attitudes and experiences that are formulating their lifetime perspectives. Christian education provides instruction for this age group with the understanding that simple babysitting is not enough! Their minds will be influenced easily and as Donald Joy writes in *Childhood Education in the Church,* "the evidence is overwhelming that early sources of consistent value influence are essential if the child is to be formed in such a way as to be an effective functioning person as an adult."[1]

Biological Ministry Implications

Two and three year olds range from 33–40 inches in height, and weigh between 25–40 pounds. From the moment they awaken from sleep, until they fall into a heap, they are live wires. They are still growing rapidly and need plenty of sleep; up to 12 hours of sleep at night, and a two–hour nap each day. Three year olds are less dependent on nap time but do benefit from a quiet time in the day whether they sleep or not. To minister to these active ones who also need large amounts of sleep, there must be a place that is quiet enough for them to catch a

23

quick nap. The wise Christian education volunteer will rotate learning activities for them to vacillate between active and quiet, thus providing time to recover energy for the next learning opportunity. Occasional healthy snacks are important as toddlers are burning off many calories in their neverending motion.

Because they are growing so rapidly, two year olds will lack large muscle coordination and possess little or no small muscle control. Large open spaces with soft edges and less furniture will provide the space they need to move around and explore. Do not expect two and three year olds to sit in rows of chairs for a ten minute lesson. They will tell you with their feet when they have finished listening by walking away and getting involved in something else that attracts their attention.

Because their immune system is still in the formative stages, this age group is often susceptible to illness and disease. Some churches have "well baby" policies which instruct overzealous parents not to bring in their sick children for the protection of the healthy children. Teachers should be understanding when children are absent and express love and concern for missing them but not make parents feel guilty for keeping them home.

Toilet training is a vital part of this stage and should be completed by the end of the third year. Teachers should plan frequent bathroom breaks and have extra paper diapers on hand for the occasional accident. Since this is a time to develop good eating habits and bladder and bowel control, be attentive to the parents' desires for their child. Each family will develop its own patterns. Your job is to fit into what is familiar for them, not forcing them to accommodate your patterns.

Cognitive Ministry Implications

These little dynamos are absorbing unbelievable amounts of knowledge and adding understanding in their insatiable quest to discover. Provide an environment rich with sensory opportunities. Say "yes" more than "no" by planning ahead and creating a child friendly room. At the beginning of this stage, two and three year olds tend to follow Piaget's *sensorimotor phase* and are more apt to follow the *preoperational phase* at the end of the stage. Piaget describes this new stage of knowing in terms of what the toddler cannot do. The *preoperational stage* finds the child learning more through language acquisition, attaching names for objects and actions. Thoughts are more intuitive, springing more from personal insight than from a logical reason. The adult seeking to minister to the toddler will rely on tangible, visible objects and demonstrations for desired actions rather than reasoning. It is easier to distract a child to get him to comply with your wishes than to reason with him. Providing another toy to play with will effectively distract them from the present activity that you do not want them doing.

Short spans of interest (two to five minutes) means that the parent or teacher of a toddler will have to plan many, as well as varied, activities. Learning is enhanced when the schedule is cycled through several times, therefore, a flexible schedule is a must. Do not be afraid of going with the flow and changing as you move through your lesson, taking advantage of what captures their attention. Because of the tendency of this group to learn best through one–on–one interaction, there will be a need for plenty of helpers to assist children as they learn. One of the great joys of working with toddlers is their growing sense of imagination. Play along and enjoy their sense of wonder for the world around them.

An important lesson adults can learn from toddlers is to live in the present. They have forgotten yesterday and cannot think about tomorrow. Everything that happens is now. So, adult, time–oriented statements such as, "next week we will go to grandma's house," are incomprehensible. Their concepts of time, distance and space are limited. They have no conception of how far ten yards is, but they would understand it is like walking from their front door to the mailbox and back. Consequently, they cannot appreciate that Abraham traveled 1200 miles from his home in Ur to Canaan but would more easily grasp that Abraham walked a long, long, long way with his family to obey God. Similarly, twos and threes have a limited conception for numbers. Rather than saying that Jesus fed five thousand people with five loaves and two fish, explain that many, many people ate that day while showing them five unleavened loaves and two sardines.

Toddlers are beginning to use words for nearly everything they see and experience. Their endless round of questions can wear out the short–tempered adult who has forgotten what it is like to live in a world where objects do not yet have names. Willingly assist them in their learning with a challenge to learn new words that relate to biblical stories by identifying objects in teaching pictures. Toddlers grasp specifics before they can understand the generality that ties them together. For instance, in telling the story of Noah's ark, a long list of animals is more understandable than a list of species of animals.

Toddlers cannot think through cause and effect situations. Do not be surprised when they do not see the possible danger in pulling the cookie jar off the counter. They want a cookie and see this as the way to get it. Another challenge for the toddler mind is that of distinguishing between one's own perspective and someone else's perspective. The concept of what someone else might see or feel in a certain situation is outside the capacity of twos and threes. Discipline that asks the child to consider how others might feel, given their present behavior, is unproductive in accomplishing the desired outcome. The parent or adult worker who distracts the child to some more productive activity will be much more successful.

Socioemotional Ministry Implications

At age two, toddlers prefer to play by themselves. The concept of sharing is foreign and beyond their understanding. At the same time, two year olds need the help of an adult to learn how to socialize. Put them in situations where they will have no choice but to mingle in a group so that by the age of three they are ready to notice and begin sharing with others. The social world of toddlers is composed mainly of parents, siblings and a few outsiders. Thus, the two and three year old in other social settings will make frequent reference to those significant caretakers. One significant way to prepare to meet the needs of toddlers is to arrive early and arrange the Christian education room with things to do that they enjoy. The experienced teacher of toddlers will not be unsettled if the child seems temperamental or fearful but will calmly reassure both parent and child that things are under control. Thumb sucking, bedwetting and showing off are some of the many ways that toddlers demonstrate their lack of social and emotional development. Patience rather than impatience will prove most edifying for all involved.

Erik Erickson's *autonomy versus shame and doubt stage* applies to this age. The positive side is that the child is developing a sense of independence. The "terrible twos" is a common acknowledgment of the more negative side of asserting will. Parents must learn to be balanced, practice restraint and correct the child without heaping a sense of shame and doubt that cripples his/her spirit. Ephesians 6:4 admonishes fathers not to exasperate their children but instead bring them up in the nurture and admonition of the Lord.

Diana Baumrind summarizes an enormous collection of research on parenting by describing four basic styles. Authoritarian parenting is very restrictive and punitive in its style. Authoritative parenting encourages independence but places limits and controls on behavior. Extensive verbal give–and–take between the parent and the child is not only allowed but encouraged. Neglectful parenting results in the adult being largely uninvolved in the child's life. Finally, indulgent parents are overly involved in the child's life and put few demands on him/her.

At approximately age three, a new stage of *initiative versus guilt* begins to emerge. As caregivers allow emerging children to assume more responsibility for themselves, children develop appropriate levels of initiative. If the parent makes the child overly anxious over wrong behavior, then guilt instead of initiative emerges. New parents need the gentle instruction of more experienced parents to help them develop proper methods of discipline for their child. Firm, consistent discipline helps a child to rule and control his/her own actions.

Spiritual Ministry Implications

In his book, *Precious in His Sight: Childhood and Children in the Bible*, Roy B. Zuck speaks of the way Jesus related with children. He writes, "Some of the most touching scenes in all the Bible are those that depict Jesus with children around Him. His words about children and His actions with them reveal His tender affection for the young . . . not only did He welcome them; He used them to teach adults some essential spiritual lessons."[2] Jesus must have been gentle, kind and approachable because young children are excellent judges of character. Jesus' respect and even honor for the little ones came in direct opposition to the values of His culture. The disciples obviously had caught the culture's perspective and needed to learn again how to react to children with the respect of their teacher.

In contrast to Jesus' gentle love for children comes His very stern warning to anyone who would draw them into sin or entrap them. Luke 18:15–17 uses the Greek word *brephos* indicating that those brought to Jesus were infants and toddlers. Matthew 18 captures Jesus' warning against anyone who would cause one of the little ones who believe in Him to fall into sin. That person's fate would be worse than having a millstone hung around his/her neck and being drowned in the depths of the sea. Obviously Jesus takes small children seriously. He even indicates they have the ability to believe in Him. We must do our best to bring children to Jesus and not keep them outside the community of faith. It is easy as adults to be so comfortable with our quiet sanctuaries and uninterrupted services that we resent the noise of a toddler asking a parent a question or singing off key.

Toddlers embrace others with great amounts of trust. While they are wanting to know more about Jesus, they must rely on the adults in their life. They cannot yet read. Children this age love to sing short choruses in a group even though they rarely can carry a tune. They can grasp simple thoughts about God such as: God loves me, God made the world, God made me, God takes care of me, God wants to help me, Jesus loves me, Jesus is my best friend, Jesus is God's son, God gave me a family, I can talk to God, I can please God, I can listen to God's word, Church is a special place to meet with God, and I can sing about God. These concepts are simple and concrete. James Fowler describes the faith development of two and three year olds as entering a new stage. The stage begins with the convergence of thought and speech. Fowler describes *intuitive–projective faith* as, one in which the child is striving to name significant objects that relate to life. He uses the example of his young daughter who, every day, would name twelve or so items in her room and would thus receive parental affirmation. The process, he concludes, "represented a daily celebration and reconfirmation that the external world was made up of dependably permanent objects, that they had names and that she, in mastering their names, could daily reconstitute a repertoire of shared meanings with her parents."[3] This stage which extends to age seven, is described as a "fantasy–filled, imitative phase in which the child can be powerfully and permanently influenced by examples, moods, actions, and stories of the visible faith of primary related adults."[4]

Fowler's findings would indicate that those who parent and teach children of this age should tell them stories from the Bible to give names and identities to ideas about Jesus and God. Further, it would seem vitally necessary for the parents to share stories of their own faith in God by expressing it in simple, concrete terms. Tell your children that you love God. Tell your children that God gave them to you as a gift. Tell them of God's provision of the food they eat, the house they live in, the car they ride in, and the pet(s) they have. Tell your children that God loves them.

Notes

1. Donald Joy, "Why Reach and Teach Children?" in *Childhood Education in the Church*. ed. by Robert Clark, Joanne Brubaker, Roy Zuck (Chicago, IL: Moody Press, 1986), 14.
2. Roy B. Zuck, *Precious in His Sight: Childhood and Children in the Bible* (Grand Rapids, MI: Baker Books, 1996), 201.
3. James Fowler, *Stages of Faith: the Psychology of Human Development and the Quest for Meaning* (San Francisco, CA: Harper and Row, 1981), 123.
4. Ibid., 133.

Discussion Questions
1. How would a toddler's concept of life differ from yours?
2. What spiritual concepts are toddlers ready to grasp?

Application Activities
1. Observe a toddler for a period of time, keeping notes on his/her biological, cognitive, socioemotional and spiritual developmental characteristics.
2. Visit and note the teaching elements in the toddler room: equipment, personnel, program, etc.

Preschoolers:
Four & Five Years

4

Jonathan and Eric were newfound friends. Jonathan, age four, and Eric, nearly age five, met in kindergarten several months ago. One Saturday morning, Jonathan asks his mom if Eric can come over and play. "I need to go to the store to pick up some groceries this morning. Why don't we call Eric's mom and see if we can pick him up on our way home from the store. You and Eric can play this afternoon while I get the meal ready for tomorrow's church potluck dinner."

"Mom, let me do it," begs Jonathan who is just learning his telephone etiquette and numbers. Jonathan's mom uses this teachable moment with her son to his learning advantage. "Come here Jonathan and sit in my lap while I dial. I will show you the numbers and then you can push them yourself. Remember to say, 'Hello this is Jonathan, may I please speak to Mrs. Johnson?' "

The call was successful and the afternoon playtime with a new friend proved both fun and stretching for Jonathan. His mother was amazed at how much her son had grown up in the past few months.

Biological Ministry Implications

As the rate of growth slows in this stage of development, increased skill and gracefulness of movement are quite noticeable. Most North American children at this age demonstrate their increased coordination skills in learning to ride a tricycle or bicycle. Climbing ladders, propelling themselves on a swing, throwing, catching and kicking a ball are standard accomplishments as the large muscles continue to develop. With practice and opportunity, the child gains control over his movements. Some more advanced children can learn to ice skate and roller–blade.[1] Running, climbing, twisting, and hopping on one foot, along with the ability to start and stop quickly, and climb up stairs with two feet, all give evidence of the development of gross motor skills. The well equipped learning environment will provide ample opportunities to move and use their developing motor skills. Playground equipment should include ladders, slides, ropes and swings for preschool ministry. A home–living center in the classroom provides interpersonal growth as they engage in meaningful play activities.[2]

Characteristically, the child's lower body lengthens and some of the fat accumulated during infancy is burned off. Normal development spans a wide range of growth. Many factors influence growth positively: genetic background, good health care and proper nutrition. Thus, the child born to small, underdeveloped parents, living with limited health care and poor nutrition, is likely to develop slowly. The child who attains his full potential must have the vital components. By contrast, children of upper socioeconomic status, born by mothers in good health and living in settings where the advantage of health care and nutrition are common will reach their full growth potential.

While the gross motor skills are the most evident part of the preschooler's growth, there is considerable development of small muscle control during this period as well: zipping and buttoning his own clothing and using scissors crudely. By age five, the child's eye–hand coordination is much improved because smaller muscles which control such movements continue to develop. Drawing and coloring become increasingly purposeful as stubby fingers lengthen and become more dexterous. The sensitive Christian educator will encourage any and all efforts to draw or color activity sheets being careful not to compare children's differing skill levels.

Because the preschooler has little endurance and tires easily, the parent or teacher must alternate involvement in physical activity as well as quieter activities. Wide open spaces are more important than chairs on which to sit. If room is at a premium remove the furniture and allow the openness of the carpeted room to provide space for children to move around.[3]

Cognitive Ministry Implications

The main cognitive developments of this age began during the previous age level. Important continuations are evident, as the child progresses to become fully functional. Piaget describes this as the *preoperational stage*. The preschool child remains unable to reverse a reasoning process, which is required for the *operational stage*. Thus, the child is still preoperational.[4]

It is interesting to note that at age five, the child's brain has attained 90% of its adult weight, while his body weight is only 30% of the average adult body. This discovery helps us to understand just how critical this time is to the thinking and learning processes the Creator designed. Learning continues to be acquired through the five senses and is heightened when the child learns for himself through discovery.

For the first time in early childhood, the child begins to distinguish the difference between reality and fantasy. In this process of differentiation, the child needs interaction with adults who consistently tell them what is true and right. Especially helpful in Christian education are adults who willingly assist the expanding vocabulary process by labeling objects and behaviors for the child.

Elsiebeth McDaniel explains that, ". . . Many teachers find it difficult to see values in relating 'let's pretend' to Christian education. However, pretending is part of a child's growth. The young child pretends about many things, he is a policeman, daddy, mother, truck driver, nurse, doctor, astronaut, and many other roles."[5] Provide settings that encourage imaginative play to draw on the naturally curious aspect of the child's expanding world.

A good rule of thumb for minimum attention span would be one minute for every year the child is old. Thus, this group is most attentive for five minutes or less while they may advance to as much as ten minutes closer to the end of the stage.

The child's limited understanding of time and space continues to challenge others to accommodate their perception limitations. A sense of time is confined to the current day. They remember accurately what happened this morning and what is going to happen tonight, but beyond that their memory weakens. Teaching preschoolers chronology or geography is ineffective due to their preoperational status. Limit abstract concepts in Bible lessons. Symbolism likewise causes this child to be confused and hinders, rather than enhances, learning. Because of this learning profile, every effort should be made to use literal concrete expressions.

Refrain from talking about receiving Jesus into your heart. The child is likely to respond, "I don't want anybody else living inside my skin." Such a response is not resisting salvation. Rather, understanding is limited. Concrete invitations to become part of God's family are more effective; being careful to also explain that joining God's family does not mean the child must leave his family.

Memory is a challenge for four and five year olds. They have not yet acquired efficient skills to deliberately store memories of past events and accurately retrieve them. They do, however, make use of "scripts," skeletal outlines of the usual sequence of certain common recurrent events. Asking specific questions about an event or previous learning is much more productive than asking open–ended questions. Specific questions produce, on average, four times more information in the response; therefore, ask something specific about last week's memory verse or Bible story rather than, "what did we learn last week?"

Socioemotional Ministry Implications

Social and emotional growth continues at this stage to resolve the crisis which Erik Erickson dubbed *initiative versus guilt*.[6] Because fours and fives want to please the adults in their lives, they need responsibilities to perform that demonstrate it. In many ways they continue being dependent on parents and teachers for assistance. Simultaneously they want to gain some measure of independence. Those working with them should provide freedom within safe limits. Parents and teachers should clearly explain to them what kind of behavior is acceptable and what is not. Do not assume that they know. Repeat your expectations more than once and verbally praise those who respond the first time to your directions. Positive reinforcements bring more compliance than nagging children to obey.

Fear is probably the most dominant emotion at this stage. Preschoolers are learning what their emotions are and how to appropriately express them. As a significant adult in their life, be willing to properly express your emotions to them. They are great imitators. One excellent way to allay their fears is providing a learning environment with the security of routine and rules. Make your interactions with them predictable and consistent.

Fours and fives are in the formative stages of constructing their self–image. Activities should be geared for success and not failure. Be lavish with your praise of their proper actions and attitudes. They discover themselves by talking and asking questions, so try to encourage them whether they are asking to really learn or just to gain your attention. They gradually use personal pronouns which is part of figuring out who they are. They flourish best with a small student–to–teacher ratio because this allows plenty of time for personal interaction; ideally one worker for every four or five children.

Their social skills are budding and for the first time they discover friends. It is common for a preschool child to seek out one or two children with whom to play with one at a time. However, they need to learn to include others and not be exclusive. Provide guidelines for getting along. State your desired behaviors at the outset of a time together. Reinforce positive behavior as a means to guide them.

Self–control is essential to a developing preschooler. Practice taking turns and sharing. The careful guidance of adults to balance between rigid control and total permissiveness assists development.

Developing trust is key to proper socioemotional development. Faithful and regular contact by adults in the child's life will nourish the growth of trust. Love must be dispensed unconditionally in large amounts, using the child's name more often in praise than in scolding. Kneeling down to meet the child at eye level reinforces the concept that they are important to you and that you want to hear and respond to what they have to say. Keep the surroundings and procedures familiar to provide a sense of safety for the preschooler.

Spiritual Ministry Implications

A child's spiritual development naturally connects to healthy development in other areas. A child who feels loved by adults finds it easier to feel accepted by God. We must be careful not to imply that God's love depends on good behavior. God's love is unconditional and unmerited. We must exercise this kind of love in our ministry with the child. As Mark 12:31 points out, the ability to love others springs from a healthy love of self.

Insights from cognitive development reinforce the Christian educator's role, be it parent or church teacher. Labor long and hard to exclude symbolism and figures of speech. Adults find comfort in both, but children are extremely confused. Just because children learn to parrot adult conversation and language does not mean they are meaningful to them. Encourage children to not only memorize, but strive to understand Scripture.

A disobedient child needs, and often seeks, forgiveness from a parent or teacher. Seeking forgiveness is an important first step in learning to seek God's forgiveness.

Worship for four and five year olds is best described as informal. Eleanor Hance, in her article on teaching children to worship and pray tells us that, "More able now to engage in cooperative activity, fours and five's can experience simple group worship of short duration . . . the leader must be flexible, adept at guiding conversation and sensitive to immediate needs – wonder, perplexity, decision, joy, achievement – turning them into a worship experience."[7] This kind of worship happens best with tangible objects from God's word to spur on young minds.

Margaret Self summarizes that this group thinks of God in personal ways, sensing His greatness. Having first learned to trust the adults in their life, they are able to express simple trust in God for their daily care. Their trusting nature causes them to accept all that adults tell them.

Spiritual developmentalist James Fowler summarizes preschoolers' faith as *intuitive–projective*. The child "can be powerfully and permanently influenced by examples, moods, actions and stories of visible faith of primarily related adults . . . this is the stage of first self–awareness . . . the emergent strength of this stage is the birth of imagination, the ability to unify and grasp the experience–world in powerful images and as presented in stories that register the child's intuitive understandings and feelings . . ."[8]

Notes

1. Kathleen Stassen Berger, *The Developing Person Through the Life Span,* fourth ed. (New York, NY: Worth Publishers, 1998), 229.
2. Margaret Self, "Understanding Fours and Five's" *In Childhood Education in the Church* (Chicago, IL: Moddy Press, 1986), 115-116.
3. Robert Choun and Michael Lawson, *The Complete Handbook for Children's Ministry: How to Reach and Teach the Next Generation* (Nashville, TN: Thomas Nelson Publishers, 1993), 67-68.
4. Carole Wade and Carol Tavris, *Psychology*, sixth ed. (Upper Saddle River, NJ: Prentice Hall, 2000), 506.
5. Elsiebeth McDaniel, "Understanding First and Second Graders (Primaries)" *In Childhood Education in the Church* (Chicago, IL: Moody Press, 1986), 543.
6. John W. Santrock, *Psychology,* sixth ed. (Boston, MA: McGraw Hill, 2000), 337.
7. Eleanor Hance, "Teaching Children to Worship and Pray" *In Childhood Education in the Church* (Chicago IL: Moody Press, 1986), 422.
8. James Fowler, *Stages of Faith: The Psychology for Human Development and the Quest for Meaning* (San Francisco: Harper and Row, 1981), 133.

Discussion Questions

1. Give several reasons why imagination and play are so important in the development of this group.
2. What guidelines should be applied in responding to the questions of these children?
3. How would you organize a worship experience for this age level?
4. Why is school an important aspect for four and five year olds?
5. What spiritual concepts are these children able to grasp?
6. What words of advice would you give to a new volunteer for working effectively with these children?

Application Activities

1. Prepare three lists of learning activities which can contribute to the total development of the preschooler. Make a list for home, Sunday School and church.
2. Volunteer to teach the Bible lesson for a class in your church. Use the curriculum provided. What did you learn from the preparation? Presentation? Process?

Primary: Six, Seven &
Eight Years

5

"Mom, look I lost my front tooth!" "Please teacher, may I have another worksheet? I made a mistake on this one." "Listen to me read this book, dad!" "I have that verse memorized teacher! May I say it for you? I can even tell you what it means." "Soccer practice, violin lessons, and AWANA all are important to me, mom! Why can't I join gymnastics with Whitney?"

"Can I have another snack? Do I have to go out and play? I'd really rather stay on the couch. My favorite program is coming on next. Besides, I don't have anyone to play with outside. They all think that I am too fat. They never pick me for their team. They don't even want me keeping score because I am the worst one in my class at math."

The school years can be some of the happiest of a child's life. However, negative experiences with school and friendships can produce feelings of inadequacy and inferiority that follow the child into adolescence and adult years.

Biological Ministry Implications

With early chidhood threats of disease and death behind them, this stage seems to be virtually trouble free. Boys and girls develop at nearly the same rate during this time. Worldwide, a typical well–nourished child gains five pounds and two and one–half inches each year during this period. Muscles become stronger due to slowed growth. Lung capacity increases so the child can run faster and exercise for longer periods of time. Expect normal variations to occur in growth rates for Americans. Those of African descent mature somewhat more quickly than those of European descent. Those of European descent mature faster than those of Asian ancestry.[1]

One of the most obvious characteristics of this age level is missing teeth. Baby teeth are replaced with permanent teeth. A perfect smile one week may be replaced by a toothless grin the next. Rejoice with your child or student in their growth and maturation.

Children this age gain ability to respond to physical challenges. Kathleen Berger makes us aware that, "Reaction time, the length of time it takes a person to respond to a particular stimulus, is tied to aspects of brain maturation that continues into adolescence. Hand–eye coordination, balance and judgment of distance are other key abilities that are still developing . . . Unfortunately, the sports that most American adults value, and often push their children into, are not very well–suited for children."[2] This should be taken into consideration when planning game and recreational times. They do not enjoy competition as much as just running for the joy of running. The sensitive Christian worker will not impose an adult bent toward competitiveness on these sensitive, developing little ones.

Choun and Lawson remind us that these active children need a change of pace frequently during their busy days. As the control of smaller muscles increases, so does the child's manual dexterity with a pencil, paintbrush and other skills requiring finger coordination. Adults can provide many opportunities for them to practice their newfound skills. They find satisfaction in their ability to learn with paper and pencil. They gain control over their voice and increase in the ability to develop rhythms that give them great delight as they participate in active songs.[3]

Among all the positive issues, there is one looming struggle for some children in the early elementary school years. Obesity is a significant difference in size that begins to cause not only health problems but psychological ones too. Overweight children are picked on, teased and rejected by peers. Subsequently, lowered self–esteem, depression, and behavior problems call for serious intervention. The known causes for obesity include heredity, lack of exercise, family attitudes toward food and a traumatic precipitating event. Parents and teachers can provide emotional support for obese children while increasing the activity level; which is the best known long range cure for the problem.

Cognitive Ministry Implications

This is a fun stage since the skills acquired are so vital for lifelong success. Piaget's *concrete operational thinking stage* appears at this time. As these children approach seven years of age, they can reason logically about concrete events and classify objects into different sets. Logical reasoning replaces the intuitive reasoning at earlier stages, so cause and effect matters are more clearly understood. Children find pleasure in ordering things in categories; arranging them from tallest to shortest, biggest to smallest, etc. They have also perceived that identity is permanent.[4] Thus, a boy with a girl's shirt on is still a boy.

The child can now perceive that physically rearranging a number of items does not increase the size or weight. A significant feature of this mental processing is the ability to reverse actions. Thus, the child can get home from a place they have just gone since they would simply reverse the directions. Previously, a child that only walked to school but got a ride home could not find his way home without assistance because he had not walked home before.

While the previous stage could only account for one characteristic of an object at a time, this group can coordinate several characteristics. A child in this stage can understand that one person can be a father, son, grandfather and brother all at the same time. Recognizing new options for working with children at this age, a common error is to assume they can also handle abstract thinking. That will come later.

Middle childhood is a time to strive for perfection. So much so that one author calls this the "eraser age."[5] A sensitive parent or teacher will honor the child's desire to get things right and provide adequate time for writing and reading activities. Learning to read is truly a monumental time in a child's life. Since the child is highly sensitive to criticism, be more lavish with your praise and encouragement. A child that struggles to read at this stage may have slower growth in the muscles that control left–right eye movement.[6] Be careful not to push them beyond their ability just to satisfy pride.

Because school becomes an integral part of the child's life, difficulties that slow or prevent learning are magnified at this time. When *autism* is present, specially trained intervention for the child exists to give emotional support from home and church for both parent and child. Those who struggle with *learning disabilities* need to know that they can do and learn the same things that other children do; just in different ways from the majority of their classmates. A much debated and misunderstood problem that affects many school age children is *Attention–Deficit Hyperactivity Disorder* or ADHD. This problem has its roots in brain function and the absence of the proper amount of certain body chemicals. Parents must not ignore or overly medicate a child into submission. Christian educators must work with the home to understand the needs of ADHD children and provide a stable and orderly learning environment. Not serving high sugar content snacks will also assist in maintaining control of this special needs child.

Socioemotional Ministry Implications

Friends continue to gain importance in the life of a child. They spend nearly six to eight hours a day with classmates at school and after school in a variety of activities. Because of their interest in peer group relationships, the wise church responds with church centered club activities where children learn cooperation skills and gain personal independence. For children to successfully gain independence they need to be presented with attainable tasks.

Verbal skills continue to flourish in this stage. The child needs adults, both parents and teachers alike, who are willing to pay attention to them as they verbalize. The Christian education classroom that maintains a small teacher–to–student ratio will more easily accomplish this worthy goal. The child is developing a distinctive personality, so the teacher must be willing to get to know this dynamically changing individual as well as the common characteristics of all children this age. As the child seeks adult approval, fair and consistent discipline must be administered.

Erik Erickson's fourth stage *industry versus inferiority*, has its beginnings now and lasts well into puberty. *Industry* is achieved by the child mastering knowledge and intellectual skills. This can be accomplished both at school and church. When the child fails to keep up with his peers in terms of knowledge gained, he feels inferior. Coming on the heels of an expansive imagination exhibited prior to schooling, the child turns now to more academic skills according to Erickson. If the child does not make the transition from physical to intellectual pursuits they are in danger of developing a sense of incompetence and unproductiveness.[7]

Worry is an emotion that dominates the landscape for this age. So determined to please and to be accurate, they constantly worry about how they are doing in connecting with their new and bigger world. Children who are seven years old worry about not being liked, being late for school and meeting new people. As parents and teachers, we can reassure them of their worth and value to us, as well as to God, both of whom love them unconditionally.

Spiritual Ministry Implications

The newfound cognitive skills and socioemotional development lay the groundwork for the introduction of a new stage in faith development. James Fowler describes stage two as a *mythic–literal faith*. Children work hard to differentiate real from make–believe, thus comes the transition from a mythic to a more literal faith. This new desire for reality comes linked with an insistence on demonstration or proof for claims of fact. They are no longer satisfied with facts that the adult claims to be true. Their growing faith may be threatening for the adult, it is a rich and necessary transition for the child.[8]

A huge evidence of growth spiritually is the child's ability to narrate his own experience. They are now able to bind those experiences into meaning through the medium of stories. They are able to generate their own stories of faith and thus conserve and express their growing faith. Although, they cannot yet draw conclusions from them.[9] Middle childhood is a time when stories are loved. These children find enjoyment in dramatic play and are highly creative. Incorporate drama activities in your teaching to maximize their interests and skills.

The limitations of their grasp on time and space will continue to set boundaries in teaching. More general references to eras and places unknown to them are most effective. Continue to respect their limited ability to think in chronological and geographical ways, while enjoying their literal concrete thinking skills. Play on their strengths by giving them opportunities to learn by experience, not by using abstract concepts or symbolism. The clear implication is that using object lessons is inappropriate when the abstract truth is not within the grasp of the student.

Teaching and learning times for this group are bounded by their attention span of ten to fifteen minutes. The Christian teacher will build on their growing memory skills by engaging in Scripture memory. Use their newfound skills in writing, reading and speaking for independent study with their Bible and workbook. Follow the rule of "impression must always be followed by expression" as you teach and interact with six, seven and eight year olds.[10]

Since much of their growing faith is expressed and understood in story format, these children need exposure to older generations and the privilege to hear their stories. They can understand forgiveness and need people in their life to model forgiveness as they develop their own personal biblical values. They are ready to receive Christ as Savior in their own childlike way. Adults need to share their story of how they came to faith in Christ. Resist excluding them from times of corporate worship because they learn much from watching the faith community sing, pray, give, testify and participate in the ordinances of the church. Keeping them only with their peers minimizes the greatest teaching tool available.

This age has endless questions about God and heaven which should be taken seriously. Seize their natural curiosity and encourage them to find answers for themselves in their own Bibles. Read to them from the Bible and life application stories that apply the truth to their everyday situations.

Worship times begin moving away from informal to more formal structures. Do not underestimate the child's ability to plan and lead their own worship experiences. They will obviously need adult supervision but the more active they are, the more valuable the experience becomes for them. A worship service should include scripture, music, offering, prayer, and a devotional story.[11]

Notes

1. Kathleen Stassen Berger, *The Developing Person Through the Life Span*, fourth ed. (Worth Publishers: New York, NY, 1998).
2. Berger, 309.
3. Robert Choun and Michael Lawson. *The Complete Handbook for Children's Ministry: How to Reach and Teach the Next Generation* (Thomas Nelson Publishers: Nashville, TN, 1993), 68.
4. Carole Wade and Carol Tavris, *Psychology*, sixth ed. (Upper Saddle River, NJ: Prentice Hall, 2000), 507.
5. Elsiebeth McDaniel, "Understanding First and Second Graders" (Primaries), *Childhood Education in the Church* (Chicago, IL: Moody Press, 1986), 129.
6. McDaniel, 126-127.
7. John W. Santrock, *Psychology*, sixth ed. (Boston, MA: McGraw Hill, 2000), 338.
8. James Fowler, *Stages of Faith: the Psychology of Human Development and the Quest for Meaning* (San Francisco, CA: Harper and Row, 1981), 135.
9. Fowler, 136-137.
10. McDaniel, 132.
11. Eleanor Hance, "Teaching Children to Worship and Pray", *Childhood Education in the Church* (Chicago, IL: Moody Press, 1986), 426-427.

Discussion Questions

1. Describe what you might do as the teacher of a middle child to assist him in dealing with worry and in selecting proper friends.
2. How would you explain the plan of salvation to a child in this age level without using abstract terminology?
3. What would you use in place of the confusing statement, "ask Jesus into your heart"?
4. What kind of worship experience would you plan for this group of children? Why?

Application Activities

1. Visit the children's weekday club program at your church. What elements of the program are especially suited for their developmental level? What elements need to be more developmentally sensitive?
2. Write a step–by–step outline you would use in leading a six, seven or eight year old to receive Christ as Savior. Include appropriate scripture verses.
3. Write a letter to the parent of a middle childhood individual giving them encouragement in their parenting, especially as they attempt to have a spiritual impact in the child's life.

Pre-Adolescence: 9, 10 & 11 Years

6

Adolescence, as we know it, is a relatively new phenomenon. The first scientific book published on the subject was in 1904. The author, G. Stanley Hall, described adolescence as a time of "storm–and–stress." His perception was that this period was a turbulent time charged with conflict and mood swings. Many adults struggle with the changes that this stage brings to their previously easy to manage child. Most youth workers take the stand that we should not merely hope adolescents will come out of this phase on their own. Some measure of perspective returns when one considers that "young people of every generation have seemed radical, unnerving, and different to adults."[1]

This is the age at which an individual becomes capable of sexual reproduction. In some cultures, the time span between childhood and adulthood is only a few months. Individuals are expected to marry and assume adult tasks shortly after they become biologically capable of reproduction. This time schedule closely mirrors the culture of Jesus' lifetime. Western societies, however, do not consider adolescents emotionally mature enough to assume the rights, responsibilities, and roles of adulthood. In a more rural and agrarian society, youth were needed for their ability to accomplish manual labor. Only in more modern and industrial times do youth have the opportunity to spend a decade in school or "self–discovery."[2]

No matter what our perceptions or predispositions are towards youth, this age level needs the redemptive touch of loving adults. Adults, of whom are willing to join adolescents on the journey to maturity and Christ–likeness, are scarce but integral to the ultimate growth

41

of the adolescent. In the same way that the apostle Paul encouraged Timothy in 2 Timothy 4:12, we should remind teens no one should look down on them because of their youth. Instead live exemplary in every aspect. Paul charges his young pastor friend to set an example in his speech, in his life, in the way he loves others, in his faith and in his purity.

Pre-Adolescence

It is hard to know if this age group is the last opportunity for childhood or the first taste of what adolescent life is all about. Frankly, for girls it is often the beginning of adolescence, thus the title pre-adolescence. For boys, whose physical development is later in its onset, this is their last opportunity to enjoy childhood pursuits. Depending on the extent of media exposure and peer pressures, this can be a very delightful time in the life of a developing child. American culture hurries it's children to become teens but once they arrive in adolescence it has no impulse to move them onward to the responsibilities of adulthood. This creates a series of interlinking problems for the individual who is in no longer a child and not yet an adult.

Biological Ministry Implications

In the twentieth century the bridge from childhood to adolescence is surely getting longer and longer. The age for menarche, the onset of menstruation, has been recorded as low as eight years of age. More often girls navigate this right of passage into adolescence at the age of ten to twelve. Better nutrition may help explain why the average age of menarche has been declining in Europe and North America over the past 150 years.

Wade and Tavris note for girls, the adolescent growth spurt begins, on the average at age ten, peeks at twelve or thirteen and stops at age sixteen, by which time most girls are sexually mature. For boys, the average adolescent growth spurt starts at about age twelve and ends at age eighteen." This places girls into preadolescence and boys on the boundary ready to begin. The differing growth rate creates adjustment problems for girls who develop especially early and the extremely late developing boys. Christian educators need to be sensitive to how delicate an issue this is for youth by not comparing them to one another nor drawing extra attention to their size.

Normally, this age enjoys the control of both large and small muscles which allow for active participation in a variety of activities and skills. Most are healthy, active, and in need of frequent changes of pace to exercise their strength and agility. Teachers should plan an active schedule for them. Boys and girls begin this stage nearly equal in terms of physical strength and endurance but are far apart at the end of this stage. The small muscles in girls develop sooner than large muscles, lending to their ability to excel in writing skills and musical involvement. Boys, on the other hand, develop large muscles first which gives rise to their dominance in athletic domains. Sensitivity compels us not to compare the differences between girls and boys in a negative way because they have no control over their development. Celebrate the differences!

Both genders enjoy playing team sports by this age as they are able to easily learn the rules of play. Their strong bodies and increased coordination cooperate to help them enjoy competition. They are especially eager to learn team games that cause them to better themselves rather than tear others down. Give them opportunities to play cooperatively together as well as compete against themselves.

The abounding activity of this group is a hallmark. They love to go places and are able to be away from home for periods of a week without becoming homesick. They enjoy making things with their hands when the task is challenging or useful for others. They love being ushers, helping set up for church activities, and aiding as teacher assistants.

Cognitive Ministry Implications

Most of this age group is securely functioning in the *concrete operational stage*. At the end of this stage, evidence appears to indicate the emerging of Piaget's next developmental thinking categories. They are reasoning ever more logically about concrete events and enjoy the process of classification of objects into different sets.[3] While many adults are eager to begin introducing abstract thoughts, for the most part, they only understand when the abstraction is described in concrete terms.

As the ability to reason increases, the need to provide plenty of opportunities for them to learn by self–discovery is important. Their attention span, nearly 15 minutes, tempts the teacher to spend too much time teaching them with the lecture method. This, for most children, is not an effective learning style and not the most productive way to instruct them. It takes the teacher more time to plan a learning activity for preadolescents, but the investment is more than renumerated with optimized learning. Their grasp of time and space is excellent as they are able to understand the chronology of Biblical events.[4] They appreciate and understand a map of the conquests of Israel by Joshua's army. Most quality curriculum for Christian education includes a focus on the chronology of Old Testament kings, books of the Bible and Paul's missionary journeys.

Their ability to verbally express themselves coincides with the development of small muscles resulting in new found abilities to write. First girls and later boys are able to write in cursive. They are eager to do workbooks and puzzles. While they have a better grasp on time and sequence they are oriented in the present.[5]

Christian teachers will want to tap into this excellent memory ability and help the child store away large amounts of Scripture. While their memory skills are unstoppable, their ability to understand and apply the same truths are not as active. The skilled teacher will provide assistance in the application phase of memory work.[6]

Their insatiable desire to gain new knowledge is partially responsible for their love of hobbies and collecting. Organizing, categorizing and displaying the items they have accumulated are all a part of their normal development.[7] Would this not be a vital time to interest them in missions and getting to know the various cultures of the world? They could collect flags, souvenirs, postcards and pictures from the countries in which your church sponsors missionaries.

Socioemotional Ministry Implications

Just as the biological and cognitive development of this group boarders on two distinct developmental stages, so does the socioemotional aspect of the preadolescent. If their social and emotional development is on track, they will have nearly completed Erik Erickson's crisis of *industry versus inferiority stage*. Most elementary children accomplish this through their elementary school learning.

The next socioemotional crisis challenges older children and preadolescents to search for and find their own identity. *Identity versus identity confusion* is Erickson's fifth stage and usually begins at or around age ten. Obviously any child that struggles with a previous stage is handicapped to tackle this new level of development. It is possible to become stuck in any stage. As we assist older children in being successful in their endeavors, we free them to grow to the next level. The main task at this stage is to find out who they are, what they are all about, and where they are going in life. Obviously, this is just the beginning of this search. Time and emotional freedom are prerequisites for the preteen to try out different roles of adolescence.[8] Adults need to be patient and not hurry the child in this process. As Christian educators provide emotionally safe zones for children so they are able to experiment and find themselves. Our affirmations of their value and importance to ourselves and God will greatly enhance their search for identity.

Less and less is the child's need for adult approval, while more and more is the need for approval from peers. Adults chafe at this process but it is a sign of normal development. Instead of being irritated by the natural growing distance from parents, the adults in the older child's life need to carefully guide their social interactions. Use this time of lessened adult approval as a way to guide children into self–direction.

As children are physically and mentally ready for competition, they are also emotionally ready to handle the ups and downs of competition. The teacher should use limited amounts of competition as motivation for the student. Because the preadolescent wants adult status but is not yet ready for the accompanying responsibilities, adults in his life should allow for increasing levels of challenging responsibilities. Just like a weight lifter gains strength with repeated repetitions of lifting heavy weights, so the child will develop increasing amounts of responsibility.

As the hormones begin to awaken, the body's emotions tend toward unsteadiness. Adults will need to draw on the love of Christ to show the child unconditional love, support and consistency. As easy as it is to respond in kind to a frustrated and short–tempered child, that is exactly what the child does not need. The admonition of Proverbs 15:1 proves helpful at this juncture, "Harsh words stir up anger but a kind answer turns away wrath."

Casual friends at the previous stage become "best friends" at this new stage. For the first time both attitudes and associations of the child begin to change keenly toward those of the opposite sex. Teachers and parents should not manipulate this natural process to build animosity between genders. Rather, help each child celebrate the uniqueness of his or her gender. This process is a natural one and becomes the preparation for sexual attraction later on. It would be unwise to either force boys and girls to sit together or to use their discomfort as a punishment. Allow ample time for them in gender specific groups.

As important as friends are at this stage, the child's family still ranks high in importance, especially the father. It is important for the child to build meaningful relationships with significant others. For the child who is from a home with an absentee or uninvolved father, the church has the wonderful opportunity to build into the lives of the children a role model of how a godly man acts and speaks. A boys club where men and boys play, learn about God and have experiences together is an incredible ministry tool just suited to the developmental status of this child. Preadolescent children tend to think that adults are either all good or all bad. This leads to confusion if the significant adult in their life does not consistently behave in a way that glorifies the heavenly Father. Belonging to a club or class is important to this age and often the most powerful ministry happens not in class but in the out–of–class activity time with the teacher and classmates.[9] The relative calm in this period lends itself to a "can–do" attitude for the child. In spite of their many abilities, they continue to need praise from adults for their efforts, even more than their successes.

The increased memory skills lends itself to developing a sense of humor. The child should be encouraged to use his mental abilities to tell and laugh at appropriate stories or jokes. Laugh with them. Role model healthy humor.

Heroes become a focal point for the older child. The admiration is often directed toward people who are strong and those who help others.[10] North American culture provides many heroes in the athletic realm, some of whom are worthy heroes and some of whom are not. The Bible presents many worthy heroes for our children as does a knowledge of Church history. Exposure to some of the great men and women of the Bible and church history is the exciting privilege of the Christian educator. Many short, readable biographies are available to provide young people with worthy heroes. Christian adults, who live above reproach themselves, need to assist children in selecting their heroes.

Spiritual Ministry Implications

As the end of childhood draws nearer, according to James Fowler, a literal faith is firmly engaged. This child has left behind his *intuitive–projective faith* for a more linear style of faith. His own faith narrative and the faith stories of others give him coherence and meaning. Increased cognitive skills make this child much more adept at considering another person's perspective. This allows him to learn and benefit from other people as they share stories of their faith. Fairness and immanent justice are critical qualities to growing faith. Moral behavior is based on reciprocity. At times, this child's perceptions become over controlling, nearing him to a stilted perfectionism or "works righteousness."[11] He will need someone to come alongside and provide balance.

The preadolescent's heightened sense of justice allows him to sense responsibility for his wrongs. He is capable of understanding salvation if it is explained in a concrete manner. The adults in his life, both parents and teachers, should be careful to be sure he clearly understands the gospel of Jesus Christ. He is ripe for claiming Jesus as Lord. He also grasps that God has a plan for his life. Fowler warns that if the child does not learn how to deal with his imperfections, he may perceive himself to be a bad person. Adults who work with this age need to be careful lest their apparent disfavor, neglect or mistreatment lead children to the conclusion that they are incapable of being redeemed.[12]

"Because symbolic words and abstract concepts are beyond the grasp of most children below the age of 10 or 12, the language of salvation must be made meaningful on their level. In addition, the child may have the sense to grasp the concepts involved in salvation—but that does not mean the child has the inclination to take action. Teachers must be sensitive to each child's spiritual growth and to be alert to any child who displays readiness."[13]

Prayer becomes a very important aspect in the spiritual life of the preadolescent. They take prayer seriously and expect answers. Helping them to keep a record of the prayers they have presented to God and the answers received is a tangible way to strengthen their faith. Prayer journaling is a wonderful spiritual discipline that if begun now can last throughout their lifetime.

Worship is more formalized at this age than any other stage of childhood. Adults planning worship for this group should include several aspects that enhance the total worship experience. Worship participants need adequate preparation time, an environment of order and beauty, comfortable surroundings, a deliberate focus of attention, songs they are familiar with, and an opportunity for solitude.

They have questions about different aspects of life and death. Their concerns regarding death and what follows should be taken seriously and age appropriate answers given. They may experience the death of a pet or grandparent. They need honest and concrete answers regarding the reality of eternal reward or punishment. They are interested in the reality of the spirit world, as described in Scripture, versus what they are exposed to from the media. Adults should help them understand the reality of the spirit world and the danger of playing with Ouija boards and fantasy games like Dungeons and Dragons which tap into the demonic powers.

His faith will continue to need nurturing especially in the area of how to make specific application of a general principle. Adult workers have a wonderful opportunity in assisting the child in personalizing the truths of Scripture in the life of the student.

Notes

1. John W. Santrock, Psychology, sixth ed. (Boston, MA: McGraw Hill, 2000), 345.
2. Carole Wade and Carol Tavris, *Psychology*, sixth ed. (Upper Saddle River, NJ: Prentice Hall, 2000), 523.
3. Santrock, 334.
4. Robert Choun and Michael Lawson, *The Complete Handbook for Children's Ministry: How to Reach and Teach the Next Generation* (Nashville, TN: Thomas Nelson Publishers, 1993), 68.
5. Sarah Eberle, "Understanding Third and Fourth Graders" (Middlers), *Childhood Education in the Church* (Chicago, IL: Moody Press, 1986), 141-142.
6. Marjorie Soderholm, "Understanding Fifth and Sixth Graders" (Juniors), *Childhood Education in the Church* (Chicago, IL: Moody Press, 1986), 155.
7. Ibid.

8. Santrock, 338.
9. Eberle, 140, 144.
10. Soderholm, 150.
11. James Fowler, *Stages of Faith: the Psychology of Human Development and the Quest for Meaning* (San Francisco, CA: Harper amd Row, 1981), 149-150.
12. Ibid.
13. Choun and Lawson, 136.

Discussion Questions

1. What physical developments determine if the stage the child is in is later childhood or preadolescence?
2. What physical realities allow this group to enjoy competition when earlier and later age groups struggle so with competition?
3. Why are chronological studies, map projects and memorization programs so suited to preadolescent cognitive abilities?
4. Why are best friends so important to this group? Should adults resist allowing children to spend time with close associates of the same age level? Why? Why not?
5. Discuss some positive ways to present positive heroes for preadolescents.
6. Discuss ways to challenge this group to strive for meaningful prayer and worship times.
7. Why should adults continue to resist the urge to teach spiritual topics in abstract, symbolic ways to this group?

Application Activities

1. Visit a Sunday school class of preteens. Evaluate the lesson activities, language and motivations that the teacher uses which are effective in amplifying learning. Report to your class your findings.
2. Ask the weekday club program leader in your church to assign you a preteen to pray for during the next month. Call the child or interview them informally at church finding out their interests, hobbies, who their current hero is, who their best friend is and what they are presently memorizing from Scripture.
3. Take your assigned preteen out for a snack and chat. Share with them any memories you have of being their age.
4. Evaluate the Sunday school Bible memory program for the older childhood department. Are the verses assigned reasonable and attainable for them? Challenge the preteen you are praying for to a memory contest for one month.

Early Adolescence: 12 & 13 Years

7

"You don't understand. You never understand. You treat me like a child. I'm not a child anymore, I am growing up whether you like it or not. My friends are very important to me. They are my life. They are there for me. They cheer me on no matter how much I mess up. It seems like all you do is criticize me constantly."

"Dad, why can't I go camping and jet skiing with the guys? All the other guys in my class are going? Don't you trust me? I'm not your little boy any more. You can't keep me in this little bubble all the time. Yes, I will mow the lawn later. I did pick it up, but nothing satisfies you any more. I give up."

The sparks begin to fly between parents and their early adolescent offspring. While not every day is a fight, it seems that those heated exchanges are the ones that remain most vivid. Do you remember being in Junior High? You may not have been as outspoken as these teens but you can remember the emotions they expressed.

Biological Ministry Implications

Change is the common denominator in this period. Change is inevitable, unpredictable and uneven. Junior Highers cannot be considered a homogeneous group, they differ in matters of ethnicity, culture, gender, socioeconomic status, age, and lifestyle.[1]

As previously stated in Chapter 6, the age of menarche, has on average declined four months in every decade over the last century. Beginning at 14.2 years of age in 1900 and moving to its current age of 12.45 in 2000,[2] the physical marker that thrusts girls into adulthood has continued to occur earlier and earlier. Most experts credit this to higher levels of health and nutrition. There is a certain amount of body fat required to sustain a pregnancy, about one hundred pounds, and at that point the girl begins her crossing into the adult world. This lowered age means that Christian educators and parents will have to teach and help teens sooner rather than later about the reality and responsibilities of being an Christian adult.

Hormones are powerful chemical substances that trigger the characteristic puberty development and are carried throughout the body by the bloodstream. The hormone testosterone triggers boy's development of genitals, increase in height, and changes in voice. Testosterone levels double in adolescent girls but increase eighteen fold in boys during puberty. Estadiol hormone is responsible for the girl's breast, uterine, and skeletal development. Subsequent to these primary changes are the emergence of secondary sex characteristics: a deepened voice with facial and body hair in boys and pubic hair in both girls and boys.

Puberty is a period of rapid skeletal and sexual maturation that occurs mainly in early adolescence. The process is just that; a process. It is not a single event but rather a series of stages. While it is difficult to pinpoint the exact beginning and ending of puberty, it is possible to know that you are in the middle of it. The average ten year old girl has begun her growth spurt which will come to a climax during her sixteenth year. Boys' growth spurts begin at age twelve and end at or near age eighteen. Growth for both genders starts in the extremities and works towards the torso with weight increases preceding height increases. The sequence of change produces awkwardness of motion. Feet and fingers lengthen before the body is able to proportionately mirror the changes. It is best to use games that require less skill and coordination. Heavily skilled games (i.e. volleyball, basketball, football) only serve to further the comparisons that are so painful for junior highers.

With all of these changes coming, the young person can become overly alarmed if not prepared in advance. Some churches sponsor a special night, boys with dads and girls with moms, to share vital information. A clearly Christian perspective is presented with multiple opportunities for the parent to continue the conversation at home depending on the student's interest and readiness. Ministry to the young teen will include teaching them about the moral and spiritual implications of their new sexual capacity and how God intends for them to use His beautiful gift of sexuality. Rather than shy away from such topics, the church needs to support families in seeing this as a precious opportunity to build young people's lives.

After external changes, come internal ones like the tripling in size and capacity of the lungs and a doubling of the heart size. Both of these combine to produce more endurance for youth. Eyes may undergo change as eyeballs elongate which may require the use of glasses. Less major but often most significant are the changes in the body's increased ability to generate oil, sweat and odor. Teaching Junior highers how to care for their bodies includes more than just warnings against smoking, drinking or doing drugs. Christian adults need to positively teach them how to honor their body as the temple of the Holy Spirit (1 Corinthians 6:19). Romans 12:1 gives a further encouragement for youth and adults to consider giving their bodies back to God as a gift.[3]

Privacy becomes very important to the young teen mostly as they endeavor to adjust to the many bodily changes going on. Parents and adults who are ministering to them need to make adjustments allowing extra food, periods of rest, and adequate privacy for the growing individual. Young teens can and do become at times obsessed with physical appearance because it so drastically affects their social lives. God offers significance to all, as no one is plain or ordinary in the sight of God; all are created in His image. A reminder from 1 Samuel 16:7 that God looks on the heart is timely for this period when so much attention is focused on the outward visible aspects. Caring adults in the teens life, need to help them walk the tightrope of knowing their value before God and taking their feelings seriously, while avoiding put–downs about physical shortcomings.[3] Adults can assist teens in finding positive identity and feelings of self–worth through various domains outside of physical appearance including art, music, writing, program planning, public speaking, service, dramatics, leadership, teaching, sports, humor or just helping out are all possibilities.[4]

Cognitive Ministry Implications

Along with a new and changing body, come very new ways of thinking and understanding. Age eleven marks the onset of the *formal operational stage* of cognitive development as described by Piaget. Similar to physical changes, these mental changes emerge over time, anywhere between eleven to fifteen. Some never reach this stage. Experts describe this final and most adult stage of thinking and reasoning to be abstract, idealistic and logical.[5] Do not assume that all are thinking this way just because their age indicates that they should be. Some teens are still thinking in concrete, literal ways. Much like Paul's words to the Corinthians in chapter thirteen, "when I was a child, I talked like a child, I thought like a child, I reasoned like a child. When I became a man, I put childish ways behind me."

"When a person does reach stage four, he or she is able for the first time to deal with abstractions – to reason, to understand and construct complex systems of thought, to formulate philosophies, to struggle with contradictions, to think about the future, and to appreciate the beauty of a metaphor. A stage–four thinker can perform operations on operations, classify classifications, combine combinations, and relate relationships."[6] The ability to understand an allegory, parable, or object lesson is central to what their new mental skills allow them to do. It is sad that most Christian educators quit telling object lessons at the very age when they could possibly be understood. Just to be sure, the teacher or parent should follow up the allegory or parable with a concrete explanation to make sure that the point has not been missed. Early adolescents are typically drawn to and tend to be very receptive to drama and stories. While sitting in church next to a junior higher at one point, I noticed how was attentive she was while a drama was being performed. When the pastor gave real life illustrations or told a story to illustrate a point during his sermon, it proved most powerful for my friend and deepended her understanding of the main point. The story made the point come alive and make sense.

One way to minister effectively to this age group is to allow them to ask their probing and difficult questions. Their questions often sound like heresy or unbelief when in reality they just need to hear themselves to realize that they don't believe it. One of our greatest gifts in ministry is to create an atmosphere in which legitimate questions can be raised and answers found without being judged by the adult present. Do not confuse the adolescent's enthusiasm for trying on new identities and enjoying moderate amounts of outrageous behavior with hostility toward parents and society.

As teens try their wings in these new ways of thinking they can become very negative and critical of everyone and everything, but mostly themselves. For the first time they are able to think in the abstract, to think about what might be, and what if. They apply their new skill like it was a favorite pair of shoes that needed to be worn endlessly.

Adolescent egocentrism, the belief that others are as preoccupied with adolescents, as they are with themselves, is one of the downsides of this new thinking mode. They believe that they are unique to such an extent that no one else can understand or relate to their present situation. Along with this often goes the false but very real sense that one is indestructible. As they dwell on how others think about them, they have a perception of constantly being on-stage, noticeable, and visible. David Elkind names this phenomenon the "imaginary audience."[7] In time, reality will catch up with teens as they realize that others are consumed in their own problems and concerns. For now, however, the adults in their lives just need to love them and pray for them often.

As teachers of early adolescents, we must strive to challenge them to think in deeper ways. Relationship building is vital if the adult wants to make an impact. It has been this author's experience that weeks and often months of relationship building must precede important spiritual growth and questioning. During that time, the teen will test you to see what kind of reactions you have for their not so important questions. You are on trial, and only when you have convinced them of your loyal love can you expect significant ministry opportunities.

Socioemotional Ministry Implications

The emotional roller coaster of this stage is strongly linked to the massive changes in hormones, body size and shape, new mental categories, and close associates who are also very entrenched in the same struggles. ". . . Their emotional inconsistency and unpredictability cause a good deal of concern and frustration for parents, teachers, and youth workers . . . they don't hide their emotions very well, even though they may try to . . . if a junior higher is feeling lousy, they'll let you know, and probably in a disruptively creative way, too."[8] Because the emotions they experience are new they are often expressed in very intense ways. It will take a little while for them to learn how to handle and properly express these adult emotions. Highly emotional appeals draw the early adolescent in and can be used to take unfair advantage of their youth. Their emotions may be intense but they are just as fleeting. Any decisions made in the emotional high will be tossed out with the corresponding low to follow.

Feelings of insecurity, anger, and rejection are common in adolescence but not in all teenagers all the time. Only a minority are seriously troubled, angry, or unhappy. Most early adolescents have supportive families, a sense of purpose, healthy sense of self–confidence, a few good friends, and coping skills in place to deal with their struggles.[9] Young people who harm their classmates are still the exception and not the rule. It is sad when a small percentage of youth are allowed to represent the whole. When one adult does a random act of violence we are not so quick to accuse all adults of being vengeful.

The most common adolescent conflicts come with parents, struggles with mood swings, depression, and teens who engage in higher rates of reckless, rule–breaking, and risky behavior. Since one of the important developmental tasks of an emerging adult is to establish their autonomy, it is no wonder that parents and teens are engaged in battles especially over authority issues. Parents must guard themselves lest they increasingly exercise punitive controls with their teen at a time when they are struggling to become their own persons. One author suggested that some early adolescents misbehave in educational settings because the adults treated them more like children.[10] When teachers allow for more active classroom participation problems seem to evaporate.

Friends seem to dominate the landscape of the average early adolescent. They fight, they form cliques (including some and excluding others) often in cruel ways. Friends are the mirrors in the life of a growing young adult answering questions like, "Am I OK?" "Do you like me?" In earlier generations adolescents once learned to become adults from other adults, they now learn adult behaviors more from each other. Wayne Rice, a nationally respected expert on the Junior High span, claims that the amount of influence that peers have upon one another during adolescence is extremely overrated. He sights several scientific studies that demonstrate that the number one influence among 86% of the adolescents studied in the important matters of values, behaviors, life direction etc. are parents. The number two influence (56%) was extended family most specifically grandparents; followed by adults outside the family, then peers, and finally the media. Rice claims that the only way that peers and media rank so high is when more important influencers default on their responsibilities.[11] While parents cannot continue to pick the friends that their children select they can powerfully influence the choice by positively boosting the teen's self–esteem. Friends are the natural bridge between childhood and adulthood. Parents should endeavor to use positive peer pressure in their teen's life. Surround your youth with healthy teens and families especially through your church and its ministry.

A major ministry that a youth group can have in the life of a junior higher is to create a sense of belonging, a safe haven for teens to try out new ideas under the watchful eye of concerned and loving adults. Sponsors and youth workers need to keep a watch out for loners. Careful and thoughtful intervention may become necessary when one young person is consistently being left out or ostracized.

Spiritual Ministry Implications

Have you ever added a room on to your home or totally renovated a room within your home? Half way through the process, you may have wondered if it was going to be worth the effort. Things were in such disarray, so messy and unorganized, such an inconvenience. The junior higher's faith development is similar in many ways as it undergoes major internal renovations. Spiritually, he is attempting to shed the childish ways of knowing God for the more adult ways that will come in time. During the middle of the Junior High stage, it is easy and understandable for a youth worker to wonder if this process is worth the effort.

Doubt is a huge part of Junior High faith passage. Doubt, however unnerving for the adults in the young teen's life, is not unbelief, but faith that has not made up it's mind yet. The questions they have are real to them and vitally need to be answered. Not all adolescents will doubt but many will and they need to know that the adults with solid faith in their lives once traversed the land of doubt as well. Ministry that is relational is so very vital. When young adolescents have questions they need to have an adult outside of their home to whom they can turn.

At this time, faith becomes more personal and less based on outward visible institutions of the church and its programs. A more recent experience of mine involves a junior higher that came to faith in Christ not because of the after school Bible club at her school, but because one of the staff involved in this ministry befriended her and allowed her to literally ask dozens and dozens of questions without being put off by her caustic attitude and demeanor. This staff person was a friend and literally loved a teen girl to Christ.

Linking the volatile emotional development with spiritual development helps us to understand that young teens need to feel or experience their faith. At the same time, they need to know that when they do not feel God or feel like a Christian they still are in God's family. God has not changed His mind about them. God is not on an emotional roller coaster loving them one day and not the next. He is ever the same.

One's new cognitive categories provide the opportunity, "mentally to step outside the flow of life's stream. From a vantage point on the river bank, as it were, one can take a look at the flow of the stream as a whole."[12] Clearly, the youth have acquired the ability to take another's perspective with much more ease than ever before. This skill necessitates a reexamination of God by the youth, so that He is, "reimagined as having inexhaustible depths and as being capable of knowing personally those mysterious depths of self and others . . . the adolescent's religious hunger is for a God who knows, accepts and confirms the self deeply."[13] James Fowler officially names Stage Three in faith development *synthetic–convential faith.* While this stage is appropriate for adolescents it is often the permanent destination of many adults. This kind of faith is highly influenced by the expectations and judgments of significant others. Fowler describes this stage of faith as "conformist" because it is so tightly arranged around the opinions of significant others that it cannot stand outside of the group of friends and evaluate itself.

Wayne Rice describes a phenomenon of apparent hypocrisy in which a young teen can verbalize very sophisticated principles of moral behavior and then not implement them in his own life.[14] At this point, the youth is not being willfully hypocritical but moving towards a time when he connects good principle with consistent living. Teens are quick to point out inconsistency in the life of the adults around them while doing the very same actions themselves. This is a step along the journey to spiritual maturity. Like Jesus, don't settle for it but be glad that they have made it this far. Helping early adolescents live out their beliefs is a pathway that needs to be lined with loving support and understanding on the part of the adult worker and parent. Being there as a responsible, godly adult is probably the most powerful impact one can have in the life of the early adolescent.

Notes

1. John W. Santrock, *Psychology*, sixth ed. (Boston, MA: McGraw Hill, 2000), 346.
2. Ibid.
3. Wayne Rice, *Junior High Ministry: A Guide to Early Adolescence for Youth Workers* (Grand Rapids, MI: Zondervan Publishing, 1998), 82.
4. Rice, 75.
5. Santrock, 346.
6. Rice, 107.
7. Rice, 116.
8. Ibid., 122-123.
9. Carole Wade and Carol Tavris, P*sychology*, sixth ed. (Upper Saddle River, NJ: Prentice Hall, 2000), 525.
10. Ibid., 527.
11. Rice, 91-94.
12. James Fowler, *Stages of Faith: the Psychology of Human Development and the Quest for Meaning* (San Francisco, CA: Harper and Row, 1981), 152.
13. Ibid., 153.
14. Rice, 148.

Discussion Questions

1. What are some significant events and developments that help form the bridge between childhood and adulthood?
2. What approach or acommodations should be made in assisting young people to deal with the many changes they are experiencing in their bodies and minds?

Application Activities

1. Select one church program for early teens and evaluate it in terms of its strengths and weaknesses in addressing the needs of the group. Make some recommendations for improvement.
2. Conduct a panel discussion during class with youth workers, parents, and your youth pastor. What can you do to make ministry more effective.

Middle Adolescence: 14 – 17 Years

8

"Mom, I got my first job! I report tomorrow after school. I work until closing, so what should we do about my curfew? I will be working on the weekends so it won't interfere with my rest on school nights. I told them that I needed to keep my grades up if I am going to get into college. This job will help me to start setting money aside for college. Jessica and Janelle work there too so we can share rides coming and going. Oh, by the way, I need to take the test soon for my driver's permit. I can't wait to drive!"

"Do you think my ears will ever fit the size of my face? Look, another zit! Sometimes I hate my face. I wish I could turn it in for a new one. Only one more year till I can drive! School? I know I could do better, but I don't know what I want to do after high school so spend all that time studying if I don't know what I am going to do? Maybe I'll just forget about getting a job or going to college."

Biological Ministry Implications

In this period growth is much slower. The body has opportunity to regain its coordination as young men and women literally grow into their bodies. Boys catch up with girls by the end of this stage. Girls begin growing and complete the process by age sixteen. Boys tend to increase in upper body muscle mass between thirteen and eighteen, during which time their arm length doubles.

The last part body part to experience its growth spurt is the head. Facial features increase in size before the head takes on its more oval adult shape. With larger than proportional lips, ears, and nose there are some anxious months when teens wonder if their body will ever quit playing developmental "tricks" on them. Helping a teen to be patient during this stage enables the adolescent to accept God's handiwork.

As a result of increased oil, sweat and odor glands, this period is marked by acne which affects a full 85% of all adolescents. This is a time for developing and maintaining personal hygiene regimens. Many hours are spent in front of a mirror, as the developing teen attempts to adjust to these changes. Displeasure with what he or she discovers is common. Adults can and should encourage exercise, medical treatment for acne and even ideas about clothing styles that enhance the youth's appearance, thereby building self-esteem.

With childhood diseases a distant memory, this age group is generally experiencing good health. The recommended daily intake of calories is higher for active adolescents than for any other age period. At age seventeen boys reach their peak caloric need, while girls do so at age fourteen. Provide ample food for teens during ministry. Eighty–six percent of American teenagers do not consume the recommended level of fruits and vegetables daily. Although nutrition is a subject that adolescents may know about, they need assistance in making good nutrition a daily reality. While many in developing countries struggle with poor nutrition, teens in developing nations regularly overeat, under eat to lose weight or choose the wrong kinds of food. Preoccupation with thinness has led many adolescent girls to experience serious eating disorders. Scripture entreats all to moderation and sobriety in all areas of life. For teens this may be one of the biggest spiritual battles they face.

Another battle teens face is substance abuse. While drug use among teenagers declined during the 1980s, a boomerang effect occurred during the 1990s. Poor food choices or the decision to use drugs and alcohol can cause serious bodily harm. I Corinthians 6:19 and Romans 12:1–2 provide practical direction to adolescents as they learn to consider their body as valuable and belonging to God. When properly managed, a healthy body is one way to serve and glorify God.

For many the first sexual experience will take place during this time. When that experience happens outside of the God–given boundaries of sex with one lifetime partner, it has devastating effects in the life of the youth. Issues of repentance and forgiveness are crucial as adults minister to this group. A commitment to remain pure, after one has already had sex is an act of spiritual renewal and worship. Supportive, loving adults will need to offer themselves, and their unconditional love, to youth as a means of demonstrating how God reacts to us once we admit our sin and determine to make things right with Him.[1]

Cognitive Ministry Implications

By this time, the mind has developed its final adult thinking and reasoning pattern. Jean Piaget describes the pattern of *formal operations* as a mode of thinking that reasons in an abstract way. It is logical and idealistic almost to the extreme. This group believes that they can conceive life in a better way than the adults who have gone before them.

Whereas early adolescents are often still crossing the bridge from intuitive reasoning to a more logical approach, this group as a whole tends to be more logical. Theorists name this thinking pattern *hypothetical–deductive reasoning* because the individual first develops a best guess, or hypothesis, about ways to solve the problem, then systematically proceeds to deduce or conclude which path is best to follow. Gone is the childhood trial and error fashion of earlier problem solving.[2]

Socioemotional Ministry Implications

Childhood provides a secure place where a child's identity is largely determined by adults. The transition to adulthood properly achieves results in personal autonomy. The bridge from there to here is the tricky no–man's land of adolescence. Theorist Erik Erickson's schema for socioemotional development places middle adolescents at the *identity versus identity confusion stage.* While this stage was commenced in pre- or early adolescence, its main work is accomplished in the middle adolescent era. As young people engage important issues of identity and the future, they wrestle with who they are and who they want to and are to become. The Christian youth weighs what skills God has given him/her with what God wants him/her to become? Confronted with many new adult options, especially those of vocational and romantic roles, teens need to explore many different roles, or paths within the roles, in order to fully develop. When adults force a role without letting youth adequately explore, the resulting outcome is a young adult with identity confusion. Middle adolescents want to begin deciding for themselves their careers, whether and where to go to college, and whether and whom they will marry. Their insistence to decide is in contrast to their deep fear of making wrong decisions or failing.

The longitudinal research of James Marcia has confirmed that youth go through three different steps in forming an identity. The first step is either *foreclosure or diffusion.* Foreclosure is a status where parental values and childhood identifications are not reconsidered but simply accepted. Diffusion occurs when the adolescents have few commitments to goals or values (whether of their parents, peers or surrounding society) in which they find themselves. The diffused teen cannot handle the common demands of adolescence. Fortunately, many move to a moratorium or official time–out where several different identities are tried on before one is finally selected. Marcia found that identity formation may take as long as ten years, stretching for some into young adulthood. Identity must be developed in one's vocation, political persuasion; relationships, cultural perspectives, personal interests and personality characteristics. Understanding these stages is a useful tool for the youth sponsor whose goal it is to assist youth in finding the will of God for their lives. Realizing that trying on several different identities before coming to one that fits is a normal process of maturing. The effective adult serves as an unbiased mirror reflecting to teens how the identities fit them personally and, more importantly, how they are within biblical guidelines.

Nearly a fourth of all youth engage in three to four of the following activities as a resullt of not properly forming their identity: substance abuse, delinquency, unprotected sex, adolescent pregnancy and school–related problems. Reliable sources state that the solutions to these problems are individual attention from adults who care and community wide collaboration. A church focused on Christlikeness will make sincere attempts to minister to troubled teens. Volunteering at school sponsored events, tutoring an at–risk student, mentoring and listening are a few ways to help restore an adolescent's sense of personal worth in Christ.

Parents and teens do not experience a wide generational gap when it comes to values and aspirations. Young men and women in western societies initiate quarrels with parents that signify a transition from one–sided parental authority to a more reciprocal, adult relationship. The matters over which they argue are rarely consequential. In collectivist cultures around world, such as India, adolescents would not dream of rebelling against parents, to whom they feel they owe allegiance and loyalty, nor would the goal of autonomy be more important than family harmony.[3] Perhaps adopting collectivist patterns would enrich interactions of western Christian teens and their parents. Conflicts tend to be more pronounced early in adolescence and by middle adolescence ameliorate some. A large majority of adolescents report feeling loved and accepted by their parents. Church sponsored parenting classes greatly assist adults in coping with this transition. Parents need to feel supported in their efforts to raise a God–fearing young adult.

Peers are significant mentors in dealing with physical changes. They help each other to understand changing school structures and lessening amounts of adult supervision. Further, they can ably help each other to find one's identity, serving as a sounding board for formative values and viewpoints. "Social pressure to conform is very strong only for a short period, rising dramatically in early adolescence, until about age fourteen, and then declining."[4] More often than not peer pressure is positive in encouraging hard study, striving for goals, participating in healthy activities, and conforming to biblical guidelines.

Peers play a key role in socializing each other in acceptable ways of "warming–up" to each other. Girl/guy relationships begin to form in the middle adolescent stage but more often relationships are formed in larger groups. Safety in groups is true not only socially but morally as well. Helping adolescents determine their own personal standards guides them toward maturity while respecting their growing autonomy.

Spiritual Ministry Implications

Middle adolescence becomes a time of evaluation, decision making, and commitment as youth carve out their place in the world. During this critical time they are forgoing a personal religious identity and belief system. How important it is to help them be in relationship to the Lord Jesus Christ. Without His influence in a teen's life, the outcome is often self–serving, self–defeating and at times self-destructing.

The development of moral actions, attitudes, and arguments is a lifelong process. Berger claims that adolescence is the, "time of greatest upheaval in moral behavior as well as the period of most rapid development in moral reasoning."[5] Combine the newly awakened sexual drives, the ability to think more abstractly and the ever increasing social circle and you have a time of great internal reevaluation.

Philosopher Lawrence Kohlberg contributed significantly to our theoretical framework regarding the progression of moral development. He focused on the "why" of moral decision making and not so much the nature of the decision. Kohlberg created eleven stories which contained moral dilemmas. After telling them to individual children, youth and adults, he asked a series of questions to identify what they might do in that situation and why. After analyzing their responses, three distinct levels began to emerge. At level one, decisions are based on the *self interest*. At level two, decisions are made with *self and others* in view. And at level three, decisions are made with *self, others and moral principle* in mind.[6] The goal of moral development is to be able to make moral decisions based on internalized moral principles. With each increasing level, decisions become more internalized and less externally motivated.

A full discussion of Kohlberg's schemata will be examined later. While Kohlberg's theory is not without its critics, it does give us a framework for developing youth who make moral decisions according to the highest of all laws, those of God. In His kingdom economy, we are to "Love the Lord your God with all your heart, and love your neighbor as yourself" and "Do good to them that hurt you and pray for them that despitefully use you." Exercising good Samaritan love brings youth to look past cultural and religious differences and see in every human being the image of God and the necessity of serving others. Too many Christian youth are morally trapped, still making decisions based on their own personal interests. Most effective in changing the level of moral decision making is for individuals to come in contact with others who are functioning at a higher level than themselves. What a great opportunity for youth workers and parents to influence the younger generation by living by a higher standard.

Notes

1. For more research on biological specifics of middle adolescents, see Kathleen Berger's, *The Developing Person Through the Life Span,* fourth ed. (New York, NY: Worth Publishers, 1998), 389-403.
2. See explanation of Piaget's ieas in John Santrock, *Psychology,* sixth ed. (Boston, MA: McGraw Hill, 2000), 318–365.
3. Carole Wade and Carol Tavris, *Psychology,* sixth ed. (Upper Saddle River, NJ: Prentice Hall, 2000), 527.
4. Berger, 449.
5. Ibid., 422.
6. Klaus Issler and Ronald Habermas, *How We Learn: A Christian Teacher's Guide to Educational Psychology* (Grand Rapids, MI: Baker Books, 1994), 147.

Discussion Questions

1. What struggles do you remember from your search for personal identity? What successes did you have? What helped to keep you on the right path?
2. Who were some of the people who were the most influential in your spiritual life? Describe their impact.

Application Activities

1. Evaluate one program that your church targets for senior highers. List strengths and weaknesses according to what you know of their developmental level.
2. Serve as a participant in a youth activity. What characteristic behaviors did you observe?

Late Adolescence: 18 – 22 Years

9

"Dad, my letter of induction just arrived, I leave for boot camp next Tuesday! I'm going to see the world. I can't wait to get out of this little town and spread my wings.

"Mom and Dad, my letter of college acceptance just arrived today. This has got to be the best day of my life. I've been dreaming of living on my own, making new friends, meeting lots of great Christian guys my age who want to serve God.

Unique to this stage is the transition from being dependent to being independent. For some this is the last opportunity to be an adolescent, for others it is the first opportunity to be an adult. Depending on the maturity and development of the individual, this bridge may be crossed once, several times or in slow increments. Whichever way the change is accomplished, one normally begins this stage an adolescent and leaves a novice adult.

The inaugural event for this life stage is usually some form of leaving home. Some to take a job away from familiar surroundings, others choose a life partner. While many developmentalists describe the transitions of life as crises, Charles Sell claims that the crisis occurs when the events arrive "off time," come unexpectantly, or several converge at the same time.[1] Expected events that arrive before or after their anticipated time bring stress to the individual.

Biological Ministry Implications

This stage is certainly the prime of life, a time when bodies are their strongest and healthiest. The ability to do hard physical work has reached its zenith. Athletic ability is also at its lifetime peak. The only group that might be experiencing their final skeletal growth are late–maturing boys. A new phenonenon of gradual decline in physical functioning begins, accelerated by poor nutrition or lack of physical exercise.[2] The body continues to increase in muscle and fat, adding weight. Otherwise, all body systems generally function at their optimum level. Many late adolescents engage in physical feats during this time that they would never be able to do before or after. Defending their country through military enlistment, participating in grueling sporting events, completing college training and graduate work, or birthing and rearing children are all tasks completed with little struggle.

Young adults are more responsive to sexual stimuli than at any other time in their life. With increased sexual activity comes the increased possibility of conception. This heightened sexual ability also carries an increased responsibility to use this beautiful gift within its God–given boundaries. Postponing marriage creates obvious pitfalls and dangers. The commands of Scripture to remain pure for the one you marry, are as true today as the day God created man and woman and brought them together in the garden (Genesis 1:26–28).

Drug abuse, eating disorders and violent death are often the consequence of being more influenced by peers than by biblical standards of godliness. Far too many late adolescents use and then abuse drugs to give them a physical escape from life's problems. The health implications of drug use are many and include hangovers, nausea, memory loss and physical harm; all of which occur while under the influence of the substance and can lead to suicidal thoughts with devastating moral implications. Ephesians 5:18 is a vivid reminder that we are to maintain control of our bodies and our senses at all times in order to please God. The Holy Spirit is a superb controller of one's life because He seeks to point us to God not to destruction.

Although most common in young adult women, bulimia is also known to exist among male athletes especially wrestlers, rowers, and swimmers. Treating the body as the residence of the Holy Spirit is not compatible with such destructive eating patterns. Young women caught in these struggles need unconditional love and professional counseling to escape.

Violent death is much more common for late adolescent males who are trying to live up to the cultural macho male images or escape family difficulties. Destructive behavior leads them to violent car crashes, gang shoot–outs, jumping off roofs, or trying designer drugs.[3] The homicide rate for American males is five times that of the next closest nation, New Zealand; due largely to the availability of hand guns.

Cognitive Ministry Implications

Adult thinking patterns are best described as multidirectional; how fast adults think, what they think about and how efficiently they process new information. While Piaget described cognition as similar throughout adulthood, further study by William Perry reveals that there are as many as nine distinct positions. Belenky and collegues report five major perspectives on knowing that develop parallel with identity development.[4] Both models reveal strikingly similar beliefs that knowledge progresses from simply receiving information from authorities, to a position in which the individual constructs meaning and knowledge for themselves. Collegians change not so much in attitudes but in the way they hold to those attitudes. As a result, they become more confident and tolerant. Our task in Christian education is to continue challenging them to think for themselves and to develop their own Christian life based on their convictions not just inherited convictions.

Young adults realize that their perspective is not the only correct one. For them, knowledge is not so one–dimensional but composed of different and legitimate perspectives on a given situation. When the issues to be decided are emotionally charged, the adolescent demonstrates lower levels of reasoning than does the maturing young adult who weighs subjective perspectives as well. An adult's frequent "it depends" response to questions demonstrates their ability to accept and adapt to the contradictions and inconsistencies of daily living.[5] Adults weigh subjective feelings and personal experiences into decisions, reaching less rigid, closed outcomes.

Dialectical thought is the most advanced form of thinking. Thinking in this way one can simultaneously weigh, "the pros and cons, advantages and disadvantages, possibilities and limitations inherent in every idea and course of action."[6] This kind of thinking is a cyclical flow from thesis, to antithesis, to synthesis, to a refined thesis and on. Each round of thinking yields a deeper integration of all the information and experiences that an adult encounters in his complex world. This kind of thinking yields not relative but progressively firm commitment to values. While this is the goal of maturing cognitive process many adults never arrive at this level. Some visit it only on rare occasions. Others only mentally process a few issues this way. Many similarities can be seen to the kind of thinking that Proverbs encourages for the wise to engage in.

Socioemotional Ministry Implications

The path for adult social and emotional development is multidimensional. While fifty years ago, social scientists labeled the adult's pathway as a one–way street, today most social scientists focus on the fact that adult stages can be experienced in almost any order and some may be revisited several times over a lifetime.[7] Despite the number of pathways to be taken, two very important tasks must be accomplished by maturing adults; the formation of meaningful and nurturing relationships with others and to independently accomplish some form of significant work.

Erik Erickson's claim that young adults need to develop intimacy or, consequently, experience isolation provides a critical understanding for ministry to this age group. The need to become intimate is essential to young adults, although it is a challenge for all adults. It appears that a social clock, rather than a biological clock is at the heart of adult progress. Each culture establishes its own timetable to deem when various events are appropriate. Further within cultures, each historical period establishes a "best" age to finish schooling, establish a career, become independent of parents, etc. Developed regions of the world tend to be more age–stratified, expecting certain tasks to be accomplished by a certain time. Undeveloped nations tend to be much less so. Socioeconomic status is closely tied to the international social clock. In South America, for instance, marriage is legal for girls at 12 and boys at 14, while in the United States the median age is 27 for women and 29 for men.[8] Undue pressure can be significantly lessened by those who minister when they choose not to focus on expected time tables. Marriage, for instance, needs to occur on God's timetable, when the couple is mature and ready, not according to some societal timeline.

The major socioemotional agenda for later adolescence is intimacy. It comes usually first with friends and later with a life partner. Intimacy follows a progression from initial attraction, to close connection, and finally to ongoing commitment. Intimacy is accomplished as young adults learn to be more vulnerable and willing to sacrifice for the good of others. The more one protects oneself, the more isolated one remains. Friendships become all important as the young adult begins to build a life circuit of relational compadres. Friends, unlike family members, are voluntarily selected on the basis of compatible character qualities, thus boosting one's self esteem. Friends provide a buffer in times of stress. Due to the limited familial responsibilities of college age adults, large networks of friends are often formed. The four factors that move friendships forward are physical attractiveness, availability to be a friend, absence of traits that would exclude them as a friend and frequent exposure.[9] When churches provide opportunities for this age group to be together, they significantly help young adults form healthy alliances. Male friendships tend to focus on activity while female friendships focus more on intimate conversations that provide mutual support for problems. Programming, therefore, must provide a blend of activity and talk time so that one gender or the other is not alienated from meaningful ministry.

While societal standards on marriage have degenerated worldwide, God's idea remains steadfast. Helping young adults seek one partner for life with whom to enjoy sexual expression, bear and rear children, and with whom to experience life long intimacy, honors God. When middle adolescent identity formation is successful, marriage will more likely prove successful. Those who minister to this age level should model meaningful marriage relationships. Observing the life of a loving middle adult couple communicates loudly.

While many friendships are positive, some provide a potentially negative impact. For many, living with peers in a collegiate setting provides a social context with easy access to substance abuse and promiscuity. True is the encouragement of Ecclesiastes 4:9, if one has just one friend who will stand with him he is stronger than being alone. Having just one friend who will honor your personal standards can support the young adult's commitment to Christ and the spirit controlled life. These findings reinforce the need for Christian higher education and the on–campus presence of Christian groups at secular campuses.

Spiritual Ministry Implications

Research indicates that Americans in their 20s do not join religious groups, attend services, or pray as often as do those in other age groups. While this may be an accurate statistic, it does not adequately reflect the impact of spiritually committed young adults on their world. They are idealistic, ready to change the world drawing on their peak physical and emotional levels. As they are empowered by the Holy Spirit, they make excellent youth volunteers. The issue is not only what can they get from spiritual ministry but what they have to give.

James Fowler claims that leaving home is the triggering event for a new level of faith development. Finding themselves in a new setting, the young adult engages in a kind of personal, background, and guiding values examination. Bumping up against others with clashing perspectives, it seems that every aspect of the spiritual domain is up for grabs while the young adult stands outside his original environment and decides which aspects of the old are to be retained and which are jettisoned. Significant adults who are committed to God and biblical standards are important companions on this journey of owning their faith. To young adults, it often feels as if they are loosing their faith because they are exercising new ownership over faith. The process most ideally happens during the early to mid–twenties. Because young adults take seriously the burden of responsibility of their own commitments, lifestyle, beliefs and attitudes, those who minister to them should take them seriously also.[10]

Notes

1. Charles M. Sell, *Transitions through Adult Life* (Chicago, IL: Zondervan Publishing, 1991), 116.
2. Kathleen Stassen Berger, *The Developing Person Through the Life Span* fourth ed. (New York, NY: Worth Publishers, 1998), 467.
3. Berger, 486.
4. Richard E. Butman and David R. Moore, "The Power of Perry and Belenky", *Nurture that is Christian: Developmental Perspectives on Christian Educaion* (Grand Rapids, MI: Baker Books, 1998), 114.
5. Berger, 492.
6. Ibid., 494.
7. Ibid., 510.
8. Ibid., 511.
9. Ibid., 512.
10. James Fowler, *Stages of Faith: the Psychology of Human Development and the Quest for Meaning* (San Francisco, CA: Harper and Row, 1981), 182.

Discussion Questions

1. How do "off time" transitions cause trauma to the one involved in them? Describe one from your own life and how it affected you.
2. How does your church attempt to meet the social, emotional and spiritual needs of its young adults? What could you do to improve in this area?

Application Activities

1. Write or email a letter of encouragement to a young adult who is away from home right now.
2. Evaluate how your church is doing in meaningfully allowing this group to minister within your church. What could you do to improve?

Early Adult:
22 – 40 Years

10

For many years it was believed that only children and youth experienced developmental growth. Adults were perceived as stagnant, hitting a plateau and remaining there for the reminder of their lives. More recent investigation has provided many fertile insights into the complexities of adult life stages. Theorists like Egan, Levinson, Sell, Sheehy and Gilligan have contributed to our understanding of adults under construction and in transition.

Adults are in transition, they are not on a downward slide that only leads to their demise. As you interact with adult friends, family members or think about personal passages, you gain insights to assist their journey of growth. "You will have something to say. Better yet, you will know when it is best not to speak. You will shed fear, too: you will sense that a Christian cannot only go through life's transitions, but grow through them."[1]

A recent study focused on adults' most important personal life investments. For each stage of life a prioritized list of the four most important focuses are given. As would be expected, the personal life investment varies somewhat, depending on the age of the individual.

Work dominates for most of adults aged 22–34. Following work are friends, family and independence in descending order of significance. Family ranks lower in this age level more than in any other time period of adult life. We will explore these topics further throughout the adulthood chapters. For middle adults, significant energy pursuing work, friends and cognitive fitness follow closely behind their investment in family. Matters of health and reflective contemplation about life will dominate adulthood later on.

While much of the insight from developmentalists is organized in sequential, stair step increments, there are some events of adult life that are not on a time table. Patrick Morley writes in *The Seven Seasons of a Man's Life* some very enlightening biblical perspectives that are more cyclical than linear. The seasons to which he refers "don't come upon us in any easily ordered, predictable sequence . . . Each of us will go through all of these seven seasons over the course of his life — many seasons more than once. Sometimes we may find ourselves in two or more seasons at the same time . . ."[2] Morley identifies the seasons as reflection, building, crisis, renewal, rebuilding, suffering and success. God often refocuses adults back to lessons not yet sufficiently learned. Our character is God's highest priority not our comfort. In many ways adult life is marked by seasons that recur in God's school of character building.

Early Adult

"Mom and Dad, Ginny and I are expecting our first child. We wanted you to be the first to know. How do I feel about this? Uh, honestly, I'm scared. Up till now it has just been myself that I had to care for.

"Mr. Schmitt, I have some serious questions that I would like to run by you. Graduate school has been challenging many of my cherished beliefs. I have met people from other faiths, and other countries that have very different perspectives on things. I really need to make some important decisions about my faith and I thought you might be able to walk with me through the process. I don't need your answers I need help finding my own."

Daniel Levinson was one of the earliest social scientists to identify what he calls "seasons" in adult life. While much more has been learned since his early attempts, he unraveled much of the maze through which adults must travel. Levinson's descriptor of young adulthood as *novice* defines this time in life as a phase of experimenting with and testing the dream of adolescence in the real world.[3] He declares that a young man may need as much as fifteen years to emerge from adolescence and take his place in adult society.

The age boundaries are not definitively drawn in this group. For many who prolong adolescence in college or graduate training, this may be the first immersion in the adult world of responsibility and accountability.

Biological Ministry Implications

Physically this is a delightful time as the body reaches its peak performance. This era is marked by few if any chronic health problems. However, for the first time the consequences of poor eating can be observed. Toward the end of the period, initial signs of aging are evident as the skin becomes thinner and less flexible. Wrinkles become more visible, and often one will experience drooping eyelids, sagging cheeks, or a double chin. The body begins to sag as individuals gain weight. For the first time many notice graying hair and eyes that find it harder to focus up close.

Internal organs also begin a slow decline as kidneys and lungs become less efficient. While nearly all of the same activities are possible as at previous stages, the body now recovers more slowly.[4] Many churches respond to these physical changes by offering opportunities for organized athletic involvement through competitive sports leagues and aerobic exercise programs for its young adults. Others combine exercise programs with classes on proper nutrition and dieting for both genders. Meeting the physical needs of this group is a significant way to connect with their busy lives.

These are the primary reproductive years. For western cultures, commonly, child bearing is being postponed until schooling is completed and careers are launched, causing the period for giving birth to be moved later in the life span. The longer child bearing is postponed, the more likely infertility challenges will be encountered. One couple in twenty is infertile when the woman is in her twenties. Infertility increases to one couple in seven during their thirties, and a full half of all couples when the woman is in her forties.[5] This sensitive, often not discussed, topic touches many young couples. The church has historically been reticent to discuss such matters. However, dealing with the topic in discreet and respectful ways seems to be a critical need in light of the great value Scripture places on children.

Cognitive Ministry Implications

Piaget described adult *formal operational thinking* as being able to reason abstractly and theoretically. Some adults never arrive at this level of cognition but many do, partly because of the mental challenges of a college education or graduate training. Young adulthood forces the merging of theoretical insights with the harsh and sometimes rude realities of the real adult world. As the absolute nature of youthful optimism diminishes in early adulthood, the person becomes less idealistic and thus more adaptive to life as circumstances demand.[6] Hopefully, along the way critical thinking skills have been emphasized and practiced so that the young adult becomes a discerning thinker and decision maker. The apostle Paul desired the Philippians to develop this more excellent thinking when he wrote to them, "and this is my prayer: that your love may abound more and more in knowledge and depth of insight, so that you may be able to discern what is best and may be pure and blameless until the day of Christ . . ." (Phil. 1: 9–10).

While empirical data is still skimpy it is becoming evident that significant life events can trigger new patterns of thinking. When a new intimate relationship begins to shape one's world, one's thinking adjusts. The young adult who experiences a serious health need will be thrust into a time of evaluation and reflection. The arrival of a first child often triggers in the adult new ways of perceiving and interacting with the world. Any event that stimulates cognitive disequilibrium and reflection has the potential of rearranging one's self–perception and the meaning of one's life.[7] Being aware of and making strategic interventions in the events of a young adult's provides significant opportunities to minister. Rich ministry connections are forged with young adults by attending their wedding or graduation, congratulating them for a new job or promotion, or assisting them with a new residence. The ministry of presence and interaction may open doors to think higher and nobler thoughts, as Paul encouraged the Philippians to do (Philippians 4:8). The Bible teacher of this group cannot be satisfied to share one–dimensional information. Rather, effective Bible teachers develop advanced ways of understanding the deep and paradoxical themes of Scripture. Discussion and applicational exchanges would be most productive to a group who most likely knows much of the information of scripture but may be struggling with its relevance to their life.

Because this age group has such a developing reservoir of information, the wise Christian educator will travel often the pathways of *identification* and *inquiry learning*. *Identification learning* builds meaningful connections with the student's life situation and experiences as the teacher traverses from the known to the unknown. Making use of metaphors, analogies and parables both biblical and modern are all excellent methods of minister to this group of abstract thinkers.[8] Rather than repetitiously belaboring information that is already within their grasp, use the available data base of biblical knowledge and life experience to deepen and enrich the believer conceptually. *Inquiry learning* happens when the teacher poses real life scenarios or creates a difficult situation which needs to be addressed. The emphasis is upon young adults finding solutions for themselves in situations that don't make sense. Discussion questions, case studies, moral dilemmas, and current event problems provide fertile learning environment for this group.

Socioemotional Ministry Implications

With issues of identity hopefully resolved, the young adult faces squarely Erik Erickson's stage of *intimacy versus isolation*.[9] The young adult must learn to share himself with another and learn to make commitments. No matter how successful the individual is in matters of work, there is a sense of unrest until there is an establishment of relational intimacy. For many, that intimacy comes through a marriage commitment. While God's design is for most to marry, finding a person to whom one can commit the largest part of one's life becomes a daunting challenge. Once the appropriate life mate is discovered, critical matters of timing press in. Many now postpone marriage until their career is well underway.

Bearing children is another significant socioemotional issue for young adults. Developing biblical perspectives regarding children will be a challenge in cultures that value independence and financial wealth. The Psalm 127 attitude that children are a heritage and reward from the Lord is culturally backwards. Having a quiver full of blessings seems even more odd to those determined to acquire many things. Once children arrive, young adults need assistance to rear and guide their young ones. Parents of young children need times of respite and renewal away from children. Young parents need the enabling reinforcement of Christian education as they embark on the most important task of their lives.

Matters of singleness loom as unwanted specters on the horizon for those nearing the end of this stage without a marital partner in sight. Stable marriage was a universal goal in the past. Now the desire for personal fulfillment finds more and more remaining single longer. The myths of singleness are many and varied. It is easy to believe the implication that being married is the "right" thing to do, making singleness the "wrong" thing. Pressure seems to come from every side. A variety of derogatory labels have described singles over the past several decades. Many are the stereotypes associated with singleness, each of which contains a nugget of truth. Coons lists five: 1) all singles are lonely, 2) singleness is filled with a glamorous lifestyle, 3) all singles, especially women, want to get married, 4) single men are irresponsible and 5) single men and women are sexually frustrated.[10]

The church must rethink its self-declared status of being a family church if by that they mean that singles or divorcees are not welcome. "Singleness needs to be viewed more as a season of time . . . unpredictable, without a specific length, and with various opportunities . . . A season of singleness provides freedom to grow, a time for healing, and renewal . . . the greatest challenge for singles and those who walk beside them is to understand the season in which they find themselves, to seize the challenge for growth, changes and becoming God's whole person."[11]

Divorce, while not God's desired end for marriage, is a reality of the fallen world in which we live. The effects of divorce are like the root system of a well developed plant. Their interconnectedness dictates pain in their being pulled apart as damage is inevitable and sometimes devastating. Sadly, America's divorce rate of every one in two marriages leads all developed nations. Other industrialized nations like Canada, Sweden, Great Britain, and Australia experience a one in three rate, while others including Japan, Italy, Israel, and Spain report only one in five marriages ending in divorce.[12] While more lenient no–fault divorce laws have fueled this trend, Christians bound by a higher law of the love of Christ have done no better. Classes within the church to enhance marriage relationships and improve communication would enhance many a young adult's life. While traditional roles for marriage have changed, modern couples seem to have higher expectations from marriage while making a lesser investment in its welfare. Titus 2 would challenge older women to proactively teach the younger ones how to love their husbands and to be keepers at home. Further, the church needs to be a place where divorced individuals find love and acceptance, not of their failed marriage, but of their wounded person. Mature believers with successful marriages could provide assistance to those in recovery from divorce. Ministry should be initiated after the divorce to the child without a same sex parent. Church can and should become a family where all are loved and unconditionally valued.

Spiritual Ministry Implications

Very important spiritual work is accomplished at this stage, in fact it is so important that regardless of what decisions are made, the remainder of one's life will significantly be impacted. This is the stage at which the adult makes up his or her mind regarding what they will believe and how they will ultimately conduct their life. For many it is a recommitment to truths and a relationship begun much earlier with God, for others it is a time to be the master of your own life leaving the God of your childhood behind.

Theoretically, this is the point at which an adult might arrive at level three of Kohlberg's moral development. If it happens at all, it will be observed toward the end of the decade. Kohlberg never observed in his own research, anyone younger than age 24 to be at level three, stage five. This highest level focuses on moral decision making that is driven by ethical principles in which the person makes decisions based on the principle behind the law. Social contract is officially stage five. An adult obeys the rules of society because they exist for the benefit of all, having been established by mutual agreement. Incipient in the level is an understanding that because laws are manmade they can sometimes be broken or rewritten to preserve the rights of others.[13]

Kohlberg's theory has come under heavy criticism with claims of subjective data analysis, the use of hypothetical rather than real dilemmas used, and failure to account for women's perspectives in solving those dilemmas (he used all male subjects as his interviewees). Acknowledging the truth in these accusations, there is still much to be garnered from Kohlberg's model. Realizing, for instance, that for individuals to remain at stage four is to lack compassion, and to be unable to discern what action to take in very personal situations.[14] Stage four thinking traps the individual into believing that their own nationalistic perspective is the only perspective, when in fact God calls us to love the people of the world like He does. Ministry to young adults attempts to produce disequilibrium with their previous thinking so that they seek higher perspectives. Giving young adults opportunity to have sustained responsibility for others' welfare in the midst of an environment where they are safe to reevaluate old ways of thinking and try on new ones is a recipe for promoting moral development. This calls for a morally mature teacher for one cannot lead others to places he has not been. "Why" is a necessary clarion call of this group. Not accepting easy answers also facilitates spiritual growth.

As young adulthood comes to a close, the budding adult has hopefully left behind the dualistic thinking that so characterized his late adolescent years. Middle and older adults will hopefully have arrived at commitment to personal faith and belief. Sell describes the transition between the two spiritual realities not as a stage but a *transition of relativism*.[15] Young adult faith is one that is not so sure any more that everything it knew was so and at the same time not sure that it is all untrue. Fowler's stages of faith development prove very insightful for describing the transition as a process of transferring the locus of authority from external sources (the peer group and respected individuals) to the internal judge who must make some commitments. Since young adults are hanging in the spiritual balance and have not yet made up their minds, "their churches and schools should help them (young people growing up in evangelical environment) transfer any authority they may have invested in their group to the Word of God by encouraging them to question doctrines, beliefs, and values and to make them their own. Young adults should be offered a rich Christian educational experience, supplementing Bible study with theological studies, church history, the study of contemporary religions and apologetics."[16] This kind of relativism is not a final destination but an important passage for young adults. Providing spiritual leadership to this group is something of a tightrope experience. Christian educators must assist young adults in evaluating their past while helping them to value it's strengths. Wise is the adult leader who plays the role of peacemaker between young adults and their parents, rather than taking sides against parents and their investment in the person's life.

Notes

1. See full discussion on implications of Kohlberg's theory in Charles M. Sell, *Transitions Through Adult Life* (Grand Rapids, MI: Zondervan Publishing, 1991), 10.
2. Patrick M. Morley, *The Seven Seasons of a Man's Life: Examining the Unique Challenges Men Face* (Grand Rapids, MI: Zondervan Publishing, 1995), xiv.

3. Daniel J. Levinson, *The Seasons of a Man's Life* (New York, NY: Ballantine Books, 1978), 71.
4. Kathleen Stassen Berger, *The Developing Person Through the Life Span*, fourth ed. (New York, NY: Worth Publishers, 1998), 468-469.
5. Ibid., 474.
6. John Santrock. *Psychology*, sixth ed. (Boston, MA: McGraw Hill, 2000), 355.
7. Berger, 504.
8. Klaus Issler and Ronald Habermas, *How We Learn: A Christian Teacher's Guide to Educational Psychology* (Grand Rapids, MI: Baker Books, 1994), 54.
9. Carole Wade and Carol Tavris, *Psychology*, sixth ed. (Upper Saddle River, NJ: Prentice Hall, 2000), 530.
10. Carolyn Coons, "Today's Single Adult Phenomenon: The Realities and Myths", in *Singles Ministry Handbook: A Practical Guide to Reaching Adult Singles in the Church*, Douglas Fagerstrom, ed. (Wheaton, IL, Victor Books, 1988), 27-28.
11. Ibid., 46-47.
12. Berger, 521.
13. Charles M. Sell, *Transitions Through Adult Life* (Grand Rapids, MI: Zondervan Publishing, 1991), 94.
14. Ibid., 100.
15. Ibid., 101.
16. Ibid., 108.

Discussion Questions

1. Why are discussions, case study, moral dilemmas and real life scenarios so effective in teaching with the young adult?
2. Why is the spiritual passages of this stage so fearful? What advice would you have for one whose goal is to assist in the spiritual growth and maturity of a young adult?

Application Activities

1. Evaluate how your church allows young adults to serve. Are the positions they fill allowing them to experience significant contribution?
2. Plan a two year cycle of Sunday School curriculum designed to meet specific needs of this age group.

Middle Adult:
40 – 65 Years

11

"Honey, our son is on the phone and wants to know if we are free to watch the grand kids tonight? They have some birthday shopping to do and would really enjoy the time together as a couple if we are free to watch the kids. Do we have anything pressing?"

"Eleanor, I am so proud of you. Since the kids have graduated high school and left for college and new jobs, you have really come into your own. I think it is incredible how you returned to college and finished your degree in nursing before returning to the workforce. You are making such a contribution through the home health ministry. So many seniors eagerly anticipate your biweekly visits to them. You deliver so much more than just physical and medical care. You deliver holistic support for them. Wife of my youth, you make me proud."

Daniel Levinson describes four conflicts that the middle adult must come to grips with: 1) being young verses being old, 2) being destructive verses being constructive, 3) being masculine verses being feminine 4) being attached to others verses being separated from them. While Levinson's original audience was male, these same challenges are reported for female middle adults. The success or failure of this stage of life comes in how much individuals are able to narrow the gap between these polarities.[1]

Biological Ministry Implications

The widely propagated stereotypes of menopause and midlife as negative crises are just not true for the majority of middle aged adults. In a large scale project that followed 8,000 Americans for ten years, the middle adults concluded that theses were the best years of their life.[2] For sure, several significant events, including the fortieth and fiftieth birthdays, may initiate a special time of reflection and reassessment. As people look back on what they have accomplished so far in their lives and determine what they regret not doing, some midcourse corrections are often made. For some it is time to make career changes, or move once the children have left the home, make dietary and exercise adjustments to increase vitality. What does predominate during this period is a sense of wellbeing, good health, productivity, and community involvement. Mid–life crises do occur, but they are more the exception than the rule. The crisis if it does occur, is not primarily linked to aging issues but more often to a triggering event like the loss of a job or the loss of one's spouse.[3]

The most well known, but still not well understood, female passage is her entry into menopause. The cessation of menstruation after the ovaries stop producing estrogen and progesterone produces physical discomforts. These symptoms are the result of the vascular system adjusting to decreased estrogen levels. While they occur in nearly all women, they are troublesome and severe for only 10%. The more pronounced difficulties of severe depression and other negative emotional reactions occur in women experiencing surgically induced menopause following hysterectomy or for women with a lifetime of chronic depression.[4] For many women this transition is a relief and not a burden. The more troublesome results are damage to bone density and the heart which is initiated by diminished estrogen levels. The increasing possibility of osteoporosis and heart attacks are real concerns for every post menopausal woman. Estrogen replacement therapy is one choice that could be made to reduce osteoporosis, coronary disease, and relieve menopausal symptoms.[5] Men's hormonal changes of lowering levels of testosterone occur in more tapered fashion and never drop suddenly. Men's virility remains constant because men do not experience a male version of menopause.

Slight declines in hearing and vision accompany midlife adjustments. Modern medical intervention can assist adults with these changes. Bifocals become a necessity as changing focus from near to far becomes increasingly difficult. Glaucoma, if not cared for, can lead to blindness. It is, however, easily cared for when diagnosed early. Ministry to middle adults will ensure proper sound system and print that is easy to read from a distance. Articulate teachers enable rather than disable middle adult learners.

The physical changes associated with midlife do not have to predict how people respond.[6] More than half of all deaths and diseases are the result of lifestyle factors more so than age.[7] The three greatest health concerns associated with middle age are heart disease, cancer and weight problems.[8] Each has the capacity to powerfully remind individuals that life is not physically endless. Heart attacks can precipitate a change in diet or exercise that have been postponed due to neglect or preoccupation with career and family concerns. While cancer was once a death certificate, it has more recently become a conquerorable foe. Cancer treatment is often severe, triggering a time of serious self–reflection and rearrangement of priorities. As the body's metabolism slows down, weight will begin to show unless eating and exercise changes are made. These crises necessitate the emotional, physical and spiritual support of a church family. Being alert to the health needs can provide significant access to ministry. "Most experts, as well as the general public, now agree that the goal of medicine should be extending and improving vitality rather than simply postponing mortality, preventing morbidity, or remediating disability."[9] Physical stewardship issues abound!

Society's overemphasis on youthfulness makes the inevitable middle age changes harder to handle. The elasticity of skin continues to decline resulting in wrinkled skin and a sagging body. Hair becomes more brittle and turns gray. The proactive adult can do much to insure the full enjoyment of these years by making careful food and activity choices. Stewardship of body and energy become critical considerations of spiritual ministry to this age. Living balanced and complete lives is something that middle adults need to be challenged toward. The educator must model the truth for words are easier to ignore than a healthy balanced life. Christians should work hard to maintain the temple of the Holy Spirit so that their opportunities for service will be enhanced and not limited by disease and premature death.

Cognitive Ministry Implications[10]

For most of the last hundred years psychologists believed that intelligence reached its peak in adolescence and steadily declined throughout adulthood. More recent evaluations of adult cognitive abilities conclude that from "age twenty to the late fifties cognitive abilities are more likely to increase than decrease with the exception of arithmetic skills which begin to lessen at age forty . . . It is not until the eighties are reached that the average older adult will fall behind the middle range of performance of young adults." What great news this is for adult Christian education! The goal is not to shift adult Christian education into neutral waiting for the undertaker (or "Uppertaker": God) to complete His task, but to challenge adults to invest their increasing mental abilities for the cause of Christ.

While the average overall performance of middle adults remains steady, there are some interesting dynamics that account for the differences in how adolescents and adults score on intelligence. Fluid intelligence which is high for adolescents, typically declines sharply in adults. This includes the decline of short term memory, abstract thinking and the speed of processing information. On the other hand, age increases the crystallized intelligence which measures the accumulated amount of facts, information and knowledge that comes with education and experience. So, middle adults are verbally and experientially stronger than anyone their junior while speed of processing and performance tasks find this adult falling increasingly behind.

Robert Sternberg proposes three fundamental aspects to intelligence: *analytic, creative* and *practical.* Each is prized in a different stage of adult life. *Analytic* or academic skills of remembering and thinking are most useful in young adults as they conquer college, graduate training and learn a job. *Creative* intelligence exhibits characteristics of flexiblity and innovativeness, the "roll with the punches" attitude that tends to dominate midlife. *Practical* intelligence is the ability to adapt to the situation and needs of everyday problem solving. Perhaps we ought to more highly value the kind of intelligence that age brings rather than unfairly comparing different age groups. Proverbs sets the example as sons are commanded to listen to their father's and mother's instruction.

As adults mature, their mental pursuits focus on developing expertise in areas that are of personal importance. The expert relies on accumulated experience and thus is more intuitive and less bound by formal procedures and rules. Many of their actions appear to be automatic. In reality, however, their actions are well rehearsed so that they appear unconscious to the observing novice. Finally, the expert is freed to be more flexible and creative in his approach. What incredible resources our middle aged adults are to Christian education! As teachers, role models, parents, singles, managers, executives and so much more they are ripe for service and leadership. Rather than perceive them as past their prime, let us begin to tap into each one's area of expertise and in so doing assist the body of Christ to function at its optimum level.

Socioemotional Ministry Implications

Daniel Levinson reported on stages that are primarily linked to specific ages. Closer to reality may be the fact that life events trigger the transitions that lead to new life structures. Each historical cohort group stresses a particular set of social expectations on how individuals move through the life cycle. The result is that a social environment of contemporaries formulates a personal "social clock" timetable by which individuals are expected to accomplish life's tasks. The expectations of the Depression Generation differ from those of the Baby Boomers, and the Baby Boomers' expectations differ from the Baby Busters, etc. The transitions become stressful when they are experienced "out of sync" with one's generational social clock.

Middle adults actually reported lower anxiety levels than those who are under forty. While it is true that more negative life events were experienced in this stage, middle adults were resilient when it came to their level of coping skills in the face of stressors. Fewer illnesses resulted from their coping ability. Santrock asserts that most middle adults experience a midlife consciousness rather than a midlife crisis.

While the physical changes that mark this period have obvious emotional overtones, the real issue is not what changes are going to occur, but how the middle adult chooses to respond to those changes. Only 10% of Americans change jobs during this time which helps to silence the stereotype that midlife adults are emotionally and vocationally out of control and consumed with midlife crisis. For many this is the highest point of satisfaction in their career. Effective ministry to this set is tied up in providing support for the inevitable changes that must take place. A deep and meaningful relationship with Christ will surely enhance the resources for facing life's trials (James 1:1–5).[11]

The chief social and emotional business of middle aged adults is what Erik Erickson has dubbed stage seven: *generativity versus stagnation.* Having resolved the crisis of identity in adolescence, and intimacy in early adulthood, the focus now shifts to giving something back by investing in the coming generation. Those who do not resolve this challenge are bound to sink into complacency and selfishness. Having hopefully chosen the first option, the middle aged adult can experience the renewal and satisfaction that comes from giving themselves away to others. For many, the role of parenthood is the means for successful resolution of this stage. But middle adults who are never married or divorced can also be productive, creative and nurturing in other ways, chiefly in their work or relationships with the younger generation.[12] With so much to give, this group needs outlets for their gifts of life, love and the perspectives they have to share. Their contributions to the ministry of the local church can be many and varied. Typically, this group provides leadership through service on church boards as well as supervising and directing a variety of ministries. Career interests continue to be important but often change in priority.

Studies across many nationalities and ethnicity show that personality remains quite stable during this time of life. Traits of extroversion, agreeableness, conscientiousness, neuroticism and openness form what developmentalists describe as the "Big Five," which have stabilized at this stage of life.[13]

In resolving one of Levinson's crisis of gender identification, middle adults experience gender crossover when they express feelings and behaviors that were previously restricted to the other gender. Berger concludes however that, "Over the twentieth century, every decade has witnessed a loosening of gender restrictions."[14] While it is true that middle adults have in times past softened their gender roles in middle age, it may have been more noticeable due to the sharpness with which those roles were originally formulated than any biological or psychosocial phenomenon at work. Men become more gentle and women develop more assertiveness.

Middle adults are often caught as the "generation in the middle." While they continue to care for adult children who are grown but are not gone from the home, they are increasingly pressured to care for aging parents. As the older generation is living longer and healthier lives, the relationship between the middle aged adults and their parents may be increasingly one of a shared and mutual relationship and not one of added burdens of physical care. Adult children serve as a cultural bridge for older adults to the society and its rapid changes. Marriage seems to sweeten during this time as the financial burdens of rearing children lightens, child rearing and supervision disagreements lessen and time together on vacations and home improvements increases.[15]

Grand parenting is another joy of this stage of life. Becoming a grandparent brings with it much satisfaction and joy. The ongoing process of grandparenting works out differently for different people. Depending on the proximity of the grandchildren, the grandparents can be remote to, involved daily in the lives of, compassionately independent of or friends with the grandchildren. Increasingly, grandparents are called upon to be surrogate parents.[16] Scripture often describes the importance of the younger generation learning from and respecting the older generation. With familys' present mobility many grandchildren are far removed from their own biological grandparents. The church can play a significant role here in connecting the generations through day care centers, hosting community preschools, and connecting older adults in meaningful ways with children through church run club ministries. This societal crisis provides one more opportunity for the church to be family.

Spiritual Ministry Implications

Unanswered questions of pain, evil and disease all push the middle adult to discover more meaningful answers to stubborn nagging questions. Just when so many other aspects of his life may be experiencing stability, his faith is either on the verge of significant growth or prolonged stagnation.

James Fowler describes a new formation of faith that is only possible for the first time in middle adults. Technically stage five is known as *conjunctive faith*. The picture that Fowler uses to visualize this stage is that of three overlapping circles encased within an equilateral triangle. This level of faith is able to examine the differences in various faiths combining what is good from each into a meaningful whole. Conjunctive faith embraces paradoxes leaving behind the either/or orientation of stage four. Having arrived at a stage in life where easy answers to hard questions are not as easily accepted, this adult has the capacity to see many sides of an issue simultaneously. The kind of knowing that is reached for is one in which a series of cycles repeats until a more mature dialogical knowing is achieved. Fowler claims that a "second naivet" occurs in which symbolic power is reunited with conceptual meanings so that middle adults experience a new reclaiming and reworking of their past.[17]

In many ways, the relative calm and peace of this stage mentally and socioemotionally provide the fertile soil in which previously postponed and unresolved conflicts can be given a second look. Sell describes a dropout phenomenon among middle adults. Six reasons for midlife adults to drop out of organized religion and church specifically are listed as: 1) empty nest freedom, 2) lack of freedom within the church to continue the struggle associated with growing faith, 3) a heightened career surge may leave less time for church, 4) burnout following unbalanced exertion of younger years, 5) pursuit of leisure activity, and 6) divorce causing shame.

Each of these dropout reasons is accompanied by a wake up call for the church to continue a viable ministry in the lives of middle adults. Creating an environment in which the hard questions can be reexamined is one sound way to increase the likelihood of continuing ministry opportunities. The church that provides refreshment opportunities along the pathway may find that burnout is less of a problem. Planned times of stopping out can amelioriate the necessity of dropping out. Planned seasons of rest and personal ministry are vital to a lifetime of effective volunteer ministry. Preaching and teaching on the balanced life that includes time for recreation and rest would help adults maintain biblical priorities in life. Leland Ryken's book, *Redeeming the Time*, provides an excellent treatise on matters of recreation, play and responsibility to provide leadership to one's family and church.

Sell summarizes the productive middle adult church environment as one which practices authenticity, encourages questions and allows for doubts to be voiced without ostracism. Holistic approaches that addresses the multifaceted nature of the complex adult is manditory.[18] He further suggests topics of study for this group that link both discussion and inductive Bible study. Theological studies of suffering, grace, hope, society and maturity will be of particular interest to those struggling spiritually to make sense of the world around them.[19]

With nearly one–half of the adult population experiencing divorce, the church must find ways to embrace this group while assisting them in reforming their lives. Our perspective must be on those that that drop out of church not just those that continue to attend during this time in their lives.

Notes

1. John Santrock, *Psychology*, sixth ed. (Boston, MA: McGraw Hill, 2000), 358.
2. Carole Wade and Carol Tavris, *Psychology*, sixth ed. (Upper Saddle River, NJ: Prentice Hall, 2000), 533.
3. Ibid.
4. Ibid., 534.
5. Santrock, 353.
6. Wade, 534.
7. Kathleen Stassen Berger, *The Developing Person Through the Life Span*, fourth ed. (New York, NY: Worth Publishers, 1998), 548.
8. Santrock, 352.
9. Berger, 553.
10. Ibid., 567-580.
11. Santrock, 356-359.
12. Wade, 530.
13. Berger, 585.
14. Ibid., 588.
15. Ibid., 589-591.
16. Ibid., 593-596.
17. James Fowler, *Stages of Faith: the Psychology of Human Development and the Quest for Meaning* (San Francisco, CA: Harper and Row, 1981), 197.
18. Charles M. Sell, *Transitions Through Adult Life* (Grand Rapids, MI: Zondervan Publishing, 1991), 153-155.
19. Sell, 155-156.

Discussion Questions

1. Describe what is good news for the cognitive aspect of middle adults.
2. Why is midlife crisis not really a crisis?
3. Why is the relative calm of this group socially, emotionally and physically linked with spiritual unsettledness?

Application Activities

1. Invite a Christian physician to your class to give insights on good health and nutrition for middle adults.
2. Evaluate your church's educational ministries based on the criteria given by Sell for productive educational topics. How does your church measure up? Where do you need to improve?
3. Make a list of spiritual educational opportunities for middle adults that are available in your area including retreats, camps, seminars, trips and Bible study and fellowship groups.

Senior Adult:
65 + Years

12

The fastest growing social science currently is gerontology, the study of older adults. Extensive study has challenged many of the stereotypes of older adults. In a recent study, twelve times as many older adults reported being satisfied with their life as those that were not satisfied. Not all older adults are senile, forgetful and physically feeble. Many are sharp intellectually, socially active and physically strong for decades longer than previously thought possible. The actual number of older adults who are institutionalized is one in twenty. Even accounting for national fluctuations, no nation in the world has more than ten percent of its older population institutionalized. Older adults comprise the fastest growing segment of North American population. While the rest of the world, especially South America, Africa and Asia find nearly half to two–thirds of their population under age twenty, America is experiencing a significant graying of its population.[1]

Biological Ministry Implications

Humans have the longest known life span of any creature on planet earth. This truth fits perfectly with how God's values of human life. Life expectancy is the number of years that will be lived by the average person born in a particular era. The amount and availability of medicine, medical knowledge, access to proper nutrition, and exercise positively increases life expectancy. Since 1900, thirty years have been added to the average life span.[2] Life expectancy for the year 2000 in the United States is 80 years for women and 73 years for men.[3] While the entrance of sin into the world and the resulting effects of the curse have significantly shortened man's life span, modern science is pushing back the frontiers of man's enemies: sickness and disease.

Many theories are being disseminated regarding aging. The cellular clock theory proposed by Leonard Hayflick purports that cells divide in the human body a maximum number of 100 times and as individuals age, cells become less capable of dividing. Thus, when more cells die than are reproduced, a variety of health problems ensue. The free radical theory of aging proposes that people age because inside their cells unstable oxygen molecules, free radicals, are produced. The free radicals ricochet around in cells damaging DNA and other cellular structures.[4] Regardless of the reason for aging, its reality cannot be denied.

Older adults are more accurately described by their functioning ability rather than raw age. Thus youthful older adults lead healthy, vigorous, financially secure lives in which they are integrated into the lives of their families and communities. Grandma Lakes served in our AWANA club well into her mid 80s. She found much satisfaction in the relationships with the children and they with her. Many of our oldest adults suffer from severe physical, mental or social deficits and consequently require nursing home or hospital support.[5] Obviously ministry to each group will have to be suited to its special needs and abilities. Youthful older adults continue to be active and significant contributors to your church's ministry. Calling ministries of encouragement and consolation should be inaugurated for those who are limited in their mobility. Visitors are a welcome blessing to those who are institutionalized. The social, emotional, and spiritual needs of the old continue long after their body fails.

Many assumed inevitable old age health deteriorations are actually the results of malnutrition, overmedication, or poor health choices made in earlier stages. Examples of this would include wrinkles, "age spots" and mental slowness. Health issues for older adults result from genetic makeup, past or current lifestyle choices, psychological factors of social support and having a sense of control over one's daily life.[6] Thirty percent of physical changes originally thought to be an inevitable part of aging are more accurately associated with genetics.[7]

Most older individuals lose an inch of their height due to compressed vertebrae and weakened muscles. Body fat is redistributed collecting more in the torso and the lower face. Body weight also lowers for seniors due to loss of muscle mass and more brittle bones. The loss of ability to connect meaningfully makes vision or hearing loss problematic in more than physical ways. However, eighty percent of the elderly experience visual difficulties that can be remedied with corrective lenses. Hearing difficulties isolate older adults in serious ways. Nearly a third of all elderly experience hearing challenges and unfortunately most wait five years or more before seeking assistance. Church ministries that desire older adults to participate will consider the size of print in printed materials. Provision of personal amplification systems for the severely hearing impaired indicates a sensitivity to older adults.[8]

One physical difficulty for women is osteoporosis which is a result of lower estrogen levels in the body following menopause. It causes the bones to become extremely brittle. Taking calcium supplements and participating in weight bearing exercises provide intervention.

Heart disease and cancer are the two leading causes of death for older adults. Risk factors related to heart disease include high blood pressure, high cholesterol levels, obesity, lack of exercise and smoking. Each of these is managable with medical attention. Gerontologists talk about compressing morbidity in adults, attempting to elongate the period of health and minimizing the period of time one is ill or infirmed. Keys to longevity include a moderate diet, diets low in meat and fish and high in fresh vegetables and herbs, work that continues throughout life, being integrated into family and community, exercise combined with proper amounts of rest and living in an environment in which the elderly are respected and allowed to play an important role. A healthy church that values and honors its elders can provide several of these important elements that lead to longevity of years and quality of life.[9]

Cognitive Ministry Implications

Much disinformation exists regarding the cognitive abilities of older adults. It is true that older adults score lower on tests of reasoning, spatial ability, and complex problem solving than do younger adults. Older adults take longer to retrieve names, dates, and other information. Speed of processing is definitely slowed with age but speed is not the most important element when real life decisions are being made. Cognitive slowing is due in part to hearing and vision losses that cause data input to be more difficult. Most if not all such losses can be compensated with glasses or hearing devices. The strongest indicator of vigorous and healthy old age is remaining intellectually active and mentally stimulated.[10] Vigorous exercise increases the blood flow to the brain, thus improving memory and processing of information. Living in an enriched environment is conducive to keeping mentally sharp. The encouraging news is that even memory that declines can be enhanced by education and training.[11]

Fluid intelligence, the capacity for deductive reasoning and ability to use new information to solve problems, continues its decline during these years. Crystallized intelligence, representing built up knowledge and skills accumulated over a lifetime, remains stable over life span. "If processing demands are not influential and speed of performance is not a consideration, older adults can understand and remember the meaning of text passages and other material almost as well as younger adults."[12]

Older adults in professions that rely on a large reservoir of knowledge maintain their cognitive agility late into life. Examples of these professions include physicians, lawyers, teachers, farmers, musicians, insurance agents, politicians, psychologists.[13] Ministry outlets for these sage adults need to be proliferated, drawing on the investment of a lifetime. Many seniors continue to engage in pastoral and caring ministries late into life. How much knowledge is available to older adults depends more on how well that information was learned in the first place not how long ago it was learned. Negative stereotypes damage one's cognitive ability only if a person fears that he or she might fit the stereotype. As believers it is our duty to "encourage the timid, help the weak, be patient with everyone," 1 Thessalonians 5:14, rather than rehearse their short comings.[14]

Dementia, Alzheimer's disease and Parkinson's are three prevalent brain diseases in older adults. While there are many similarities in the symptomology of these conditions, each has its own identifying characteristics. Dementia patients experience severely impaired judgment, memory or problem solving ability. More than fifty diseases can trigger the disease. All forms are chronic, most are degenerative.[15] Alzheimer's is best described as a progressive irreversible brain disorder that is characterized by gradual deterioration of memory, reasoning, language, and eventually physically functioning.[16] During early stages of the disease, family members are often able to provide the needed support but as the disease progresses full–time care becomes a necessity. The affected person eventually lives in a state of total dependency.[17] Parkinson's chronic progressive disease is most noticeable in muscle tremors and rigidity. Compassion, support, and consistent loving are needed by both those experiencing these conditions as well as the family who care for their daily needs. Chronic conditions tax the body, its immune system and drain both financial and emotional reservoirs of all concerned. Christians need to demonstrate their depth of caring to those affected.

Older adults combine wisdom with increasing aesthetic sensitivity and life reflections. All three increase with age! Aesthetic sense is heightened in seniors appreciating and enjoying nature as never before.[18] Life review involves the examination of one's own past, which is not only therapeutic for the older person but a superb reservoir of insight for the younger generations. Wisdom intertwines a lifetime of knowledge with the practical aspects of life. While a build up of life experiences is prerequest to wisdom, age is not a guarantee. Solomon was right when he encouraged youth to, "pursue wisdom as you pursue silver and gold . . ."

Socioemotional Ministry Implications

The key to satisfaction and sense of well being in older adults is summarized in the activity theory. The more active and involved older people are, the more satisfied they are and the more likely they will stay healthy, go to church, attend meetings, and take trips. Those who make healthy choices regarding exercise are happier than those who sit at home. Ministry to this group can and should provide opportunities to be socially active. With less responsibilities at home, this group is free to travel and explore. Many churches have formed monthly times where older adults gather to share a meal and a devotional time. An outreach oriented church uses social and travel times to minister to unchurched community adults.[19]

Erik Erickson described this as the time to experience either ego integrity or resign oneself to despair. His eighth stage finds older people striving to reach the ultimate goal of wisdom, spiritual tranquility, and an acceptance of their lives. As a healthy child will not fear life, so a healthy adult will not fear death.[20] For the Christian, the end of this life is just the beginning of a better existence in heaven with a loving, caring heavenly Father. For the unbeliever, the end of this life means meeting your maker and giving an account of all that you have done and being judged accordingly. Fear is an appropriate response for those without Christ as they face the end of their earthly existence. The good news is that while they have breath they can still make a decision to surrender to God.

"Life is lived forward but understood backward" claimed Soren Kierkegaard. Thus older adulthood becomes a time to look back and evaluate one's life journey. The retrospective glance can be positive resulting in a sense of integrity or negative resulting in a sense of despair. Emotionally this stage is described in terms of success not decline; especially for those that make wise choices regarding proper diet, exercise, mental stimulation, good social relationships, and support and absence of disease. Having made wise decisions in these areas, an older adult finds that many abilities decline very slowly. The key is simple: choose the active life over the passive life to help slow the rate of aging.[21]

One of the troubling emotional aspects of this age group is depression. Sometimes misdiagnosed as dementia, the real struggle for many is depression. Proper help that can be gained through medication and counseling. On the whole it seems that depression causes intellectual decline more often than declines in intellectual ability affect mood.[22] Depression and passivity are not inevitable. They are often a result of the loss of meaningful activity and control over the events of one's life.[23] Family and care takers can greatly assist those struggling with depression by treating them with respect and by giving these individuals as much control over their life and decisions as is humanly possible. Those adults who are able to cultivate resilient ability to bounce back after life's losses and stresses are those whose well–being improves. Life will bring emotional challenges but faith in God definitely gives one resiliency. Think on these things . . . (Philippians 4:7–8).

Dealing with loss is a significant aspect of older adulthood. Older adults first deal with the loss of close friends and possibly a spouse. This serves as prelude to their own mortality. Elizabeth Kubler–Ross described five stages through which individuals transverse when facing and dealing with death. Those stages are *denial and isolation, anger, bargaining, depression,* and *acceptance.* Not all of the stages are accomplished in lockstep order. Not all of the stages are experienced by all, but Kubler–Ross's paradigm provides helpful insights for those who are coming alongside to assist those experiencing loss. Widows outnumber widowers five to one. This is true because women live longer, marry older men, and widower's tend to remarry while widows do not. Widowed women constitute the poorest group in America. The less educated they are the more they experience loneliness.[24] Presenting the good news of Christ's work on the cross in paying the price of redemption is the best news that can be shared with those who are grieving. Loosing a mate creates real pain. What older adults need much more than a sermon is a companion with whom to share their thoughts and memories. Listening to the grieving may be the most significant ministry one can offer.

Wiebe challenges older adults to say goodbye to the reality of enjoying complete independence until one dies, to the dreams of previous stages of life without feeling guilt, failure, or despondency; to the need to control adult children and to the world of work. On the other side of the coin she entreats adults to cherish and embrace the "hello's" of this time of life. Among them she names saying hello to meaning through being rather than doing, hello to freedom from competition in the work world and wearying schedules, hello to the opportunity to give back to society lessons, resources, and experiences harvested over a lifetime, and hello to finding an even stronger basis for your beliefs.[25]

Spiritual Ministry Implications

Scripture has much to say on the topic of growing older. Lost by Western culture, but vital to biblical ideals and standards is the practice of respecting the wisdom and goodness of elders (Leviticus 19:32, Prov.20:29, Job 32:6, 7 among others). Long and satisfying life rewards the one who is obedient to God's word (Ephesians 6:2, Prov. 3:1,2). Old age continues to be a time of service and fruit bearing for many whose stories are told in holy writ including David (Ps. 92:14), Caleb (Joshua 14:12), church leaders (Titus 1:5, 1 Timothy 5:9–10, Titus 2:1–5), and Anna and Simeon (Luke 2:25–38). Old age is a time to bless others and release one's grip on life. Elijah blessed and commissioned Elisha (2 Kings 2:11) in his final hours. Jacob gathered his sons and gave them a personal and meaningful blessing before his passing (Genesis 49:28). Paul passed the torch of responsibility onto Timothy in his farewell letter from prison (2 Timothy 4:1–8). Surely we have many godly examples of how to navigate this final passage.

"Our goal, therefore is to educate and inspire middle and older adults in the faith community to see aging as a process that is both challenging and graceful . . . The good news of the gospel should mean hope and grace for older adults, regardless of their circumstances. This book is . . . a challenge to achieve meaning, maintain hope, and continue to serve, through being and doing as long as possible and solely through being as the years advance."[26] Katie Wiebe continues by characterizing senior adults as a group booming in numbers, living longer, feeling younger, better informed and more traveled than ever before. Their challenge is to reshape moral and ethical values, influence medical ethics, to strengthen family life and to teach others to accept death as a part of the life cycle. This is a tall order and is surely not a time to slow down; shift gears maybe, but quit . . . never!

Due to mandatory retirement laws being declared illegal, many are working longer and enjoying it more. For those who choose either partial or complete retirement, there exists a need to meaningfully give themselves away to the next generation in what social scientists describe as generatively. Volunteerism is increasing both in quantity and quality as seniors contribute their valuable skills, love and time. The church can act as a networking center meaningfully connecting people with time, love, and wisdom with those that need it. Seniors can serve as foster grandparents, tutors, a friendly voice for latchkey kids, or volunteers in children's and youth ministries. Many seniors provide leadership on church boards, on church committees, and as directors of various church ministries. James Waltner describes the vast reservoir of resources that the older church adults are. "They can engage in public and private prayer, teach, visit, improve and maintain church property, do clerical work, child care, work as community service volunteers, counsel, and help in countless other ways."[27] Waltner describes effective ministry to this group as being literally a "hands–on" endeavor with lots of time and opportunities to exchange hugs and give physical support.

Another spiritual gift that those finishing life have to give is their story. Helen Alderfer claims that in telling one's story, the elderly build a continuity with the past, share their faith, follow a biblical pattern and experience psychological healing. She challenges older adults to tell their stories verbally, on video or audio tape recording, through journaling of all kinds. Through letter writing to grandchildren and children, seniors can share the day–to–day things that they believe, how they deal with life's experiences, crises events being sure to include both the "inner and outer weather" aspects.[28]

HOPE! That's the message that older adults need to know, live and pass on to others! In personal interviews with over seventy eighty year old adults, Paul Miller asked them to share how their childhood hopes were challenged in life and what they now hoped for at age eighty. All of the interviewees reflected on their childhood faith shared with them by their mothers. Many focused on the ability to expect undeserved grace throughout life. Remaining faithful to God amid trials and reverses was a recurent theme. Many mentioned using one's life as a peacemaker. Others encouraged choosing humor and positive attitude. Having a deep spiritual life and enjoying both the biological family and the faith family as you journey toward heaven were central responses as well.[29]

Notes

1. Kathleen Stassen Berger, *The Developing Person Through the Life Span*, fourth ed. (New York, NY: Worth Publishers, 1998), 605-606.
2. John Santrock, *Psychology*, sixth ed. (Boston, MA: McGraw Hill, 2000), 353.
3. Ibid.
4. Ibid., 354.
5. Berger, 606.
6. Ibid., 613-614.
7. Carole Wade and Carol Tavris, *Psychology*, sixth ed. (Upper Saddle River, NJ: Prentice Hall, 2000), 536.
8. Berger, 611-612.
9. Ibid., 615-626.
10. Wade, 536.
11. John Santrock, *Psychology*, sixth ed. (Boston, MA: McGraw Hill, 2000), 356.
12. Berger, 634.
13. Wade, 535.
14. Berger, 637 & 642.
15. Ibid., 645.
16. Santrock, 354.
17. Berger, 648.
18. Ibid., 654.
19. Santrock, 359.
20. Wade, 530.
21. Santrock, 360.
22. Berger, 652.
23. Wade, 536.
24. Santrock, 362.
25. Katie FunkWiebe, authored various sections of (see Bibliography for specifics), *Life After 50: A Positive Look at Aging in the Faith Community* (Newton, KS: Faith and Life Press, 1993), 69-75.
26. Ibid., VIII.

27. James H. Waltner, "Who Will Be With Me When I Am Old?", in *Life After 50: A Positive Look at Aging in the Faith Community* (Newton, KS: Faith and Life Press, 1993), 121.

28. Helen Wade Alderfer, "You Have a Story to Tell", in *Life After 50: A Positive Look at Aging in the Faith Community* (Newton, KS: Faith and Life Press, 1993), 128-138.

29. Paul M. Miller, "Aging with Hope in the Faith Community", in *Life After 50: A Positive Look at Aging in the Faith Community* (Newton, KS: Faith and Life Press, 1993), 153-164.

Discussion Questions

1. What misconceptions have you embraced? What new insights have you learned about the physical prowess of older adults?
2. What changes in your lifestyle should you consider making right now that could enhance your later years?
3. Whom do you know with excellent crystallized intelligence? What makes you think that?
4. Whom do you know that ended their years with integrity? What contributed to that end?
5. List ways that older adults contribute to your church family. Create a second list of ways that you think they could be more usefully engaged in ministry.

Application Activities

1. Skim read *Transitions Through Adult Life* by Charles Sell and report to the class three significant findings.
2. Contact a local Christian camp asking what ministries they use to target the older adult.
3. Volunteer in a local senior center, engaging in conversation with three octagenarians. Find out what they value about their life. What advice would they give to middle adults?
4. Contact a senior adult and volunteer to write part of his/her spiritual story for him/her. Share your work with the class.
5. Call your grandparent and ask him/her to tell you what they have learned about life, serving God and enjoying life?

Bibliography

Alderfer, Helen Wade. "You Have a Story to Tell", in *Life After 50: A Positive Look at Aging in the Faith Community*. Newton, KS: Faith and Life Press, 1993.

Berger, Kathleen Stassen. *The Developing Person Through the Life Span*, fourth ed. New York, NY: Worth Publishers, 1998.

Bufford, Bob. *Halftime: Changing Your Game Plan from Success to Significance*. Grand Rapids, MI: Zondervan Publishing, 1994.

Butman, Richard E. and Moore, David R. "The Power of Perry and Belenky", in *Nurture that is Christian: Developmental Perspectives on Christian Education*, ed. James C. Wilhoit and John M. Dettoni. Grand Rapids, MI: Harper and Row, 1998.

Choun, Robert and Lawson, Michael. *The Complete Handbook for Children's Ministry: How to Reach and Teach the Next Generation*. Nashville, TN: Thomas Nelson Publishers, 1993.

Coons, Carolyn. Fagerstrom, Douglas, ed."Today's Single Adult Phenomenon: The Realities and Myths", in *Singles Ministry Handbook: A Practical Guide to Reaching Adult Singles in the Church*. Wheaton, IL: Victor Books, 1988.

Cox, Harold, ed. *Aging*. twelveth ed. Guilford, CT: Annual Editions of Dushkin/McGraw Hill, 1998-1999.

Eberle, Sarah. "Understanding Third and Fourth Graders" (Middlers), *Childhood Education in the Church*. Chicago, IL: Moody Press, 1986.

Fowler, James. *Stages of Faith: the Psychology of Human Development and the Quest for Meaning*. San Francisco, CA: Harper and Row, 1981.

Freudenburg, Ben and Lawrence, Rick. *The Family Friendly Church*. Loveland, CO: Vital Ministry with Group Publishing, 1998.

Gangel, Kenneth O. and Wilhoit James C. ed. *The Christian Educator's Handbook of Family Life Education*. Grand Rapids, MI: Baker Books, 1996.

Hance, Eleanor. "Teaching Children to Worship and Pray", in *Childhood Education in the Church*. Chicago IL: Moody Press, 1986.

Haystead, Wesley. *Teaching Your Child About God: How to Establish and Nurture Your Child's Relationship with God*. Ventura, CA: Regal Books, 1995.

Issler, Klaus and Habermas, Ronald. *How We Learn: A Christian Teacher's Guide to Educational Psychology*. Grand Rapids, MI: Baker Books, 1994.

Joy, Donald. "Why Reach and Teach Children?", in *Childhood Education in the Church*, ed. by Robert Clark, Joanne Brubaker, Roy Zuck. Chicago, IL: Moody Press, 1986.

Junn, Ellen and Boyatzis, Chris J. *Child Growth and Development*, sixth ed. Guilford, CT: Annual Editions of Dushkin/McGraw Hill, 1999-2000.

Levinson, Daniel J. *The Seasons of a Man's Life*. New York, NY: Ballantine Books, 1978.

McDaniel, Elsiebeth. "Understanding First and Second Graders" (Primaries), in *Childhood Education in the Church*. Chicago, IL: Moody Press, 1986.

McDowell, Josh and Hostetler, Bob. *Handbook on Counseling Youth: A Comprehensive Guide for Equipping Youth Workers, Pastors, Teachers, Parents*. Dallas, TX: Word Publishing Co., 1996.

Meehan, Anita A. and Astor-Stetson, Eileen, ed. *Adolescent Psychology*, second ed. Guilford, CT: Annual Editions of Dushkin/McGraw Hill, 1998-1999.

Miller, Paul M. "Aging with Hope in the Faith Community", in *Life After 50: A Positive Look at Aging in the Faith Community*. Newton, KS: Faith and Life Press, 1993.

Mueller, Walt. *Understanding Today's Youth Culture*. Wheaton, IL: Tyndale Publishing House, 1999.

Rice, Wayne. *Junior High Ministry: A Guide to Early Adolescence for Youth Workers*. Grand Rapids, MI: Zondervan Publishing, 1998.

Santrock, John W. *Psychology*, sixth ed. Boston, MA: McGraw Hill, 2000.

Self, Margaret. "Understanding Four's and Five's", *In Childhood Education in the Church*. Chicago, IL: Moody Press, 1986.

Soderholm, Marjorie. "Understanding Fifth and Sixth Graders" (Juniors), in *Childhood Education in the Church*, ed. Clark, Brubaker, Zuck. Chicago, IL: Moody Press, 1986.

Stonehouse, Catherine. *Joining Children on the Spiritual Journey: Nurturing a Life of Faith*. Grand Rapids, MI: Baker Books, 1998.

Wade, Carole and Tavris, Carol. *Psychology*, sixth ed. Upper Saddle River, NJ: Prentice Hall, 2000.

Waltner, James H. "Who Will Be With Me When I Am Old?", in *Life After 50: A Positive Look at Aging in the Faith Community*. Newton, KS: Faith and Life Press, 1993.

Wiebe, Katie Funk. "If You're Going To Be Old, Now is the Time", "What the Bible Tells Us About Growing Older", "Turning Losses Into Gains: It Is Possible!", in *Life After 50: A Positive Look at Aging in the Faith Community*. Newton, KS: Faith and Life Press, 1993.

Wilhoit, James C. and Dettoni, John M., ed. *Nurture That Is Christian: Developmental Perspectives on Christian Education*. Grand Rapids, MI: Baker Books, 1998.

Wilson, Fred. "Adult Development", in *Nurture That Is Christian: Developmental Perspectives on Chrisitan Education*, ed. Wilhoit and Dettoni. Grand Rapids, MI: Baker Books, 1998.